To Indigenous children throughout the world, who have lost their cultural and spiritual heritage to colonization, epistemicide and genocide, resulting in pandemic historical trauma and inter-generational trauma transmission.

May we begin to rebuild what has been lost one generation at a time…

Copyright © 2017 by Carey MacCarthy & Linda Chapman

All rights reserved
Printed in The United States of America
First Edition

For information about permission to reproduce selections from this book, please write to:

Carey MacCarthy 10 Santa Margarita Dr. San Rafael, CA 94901
carey@indigenoushealingarts.org

Linda Chapman 10151 East Rd, Redwood Valley, CA 95470
arttherapy@pacific.net

Library of Congress Cataloging-in-publishing Data

MacCarthy, Carey 1972-

Chapman, Linda 1951-

Library of Congress Control Number: 2017916419
CreateSpace Independent Publishing Platform, North Charleston, SC

Start UP! ©: A School-Based Arts Curriculum for Native American Youth and All Cultures: Interventions for Development and Learning – First Edition.

ISBN-13:
978-1978144033

ISBN-10:
1978144032

Indigenous Healing Arts Alliance –Self Published through Amazon, Create Space
First Edition 2017

Indigenous Healing Arts Alliance

START UP!

A School-Based Arts Curriculum for Native American Youth and All Cultures: Interventions for Development and Learning

FACILITATORS MANUAL

Carey MacCarthy, MA, ATR-LPCC
Linda Chapman, MA, ATR-BC

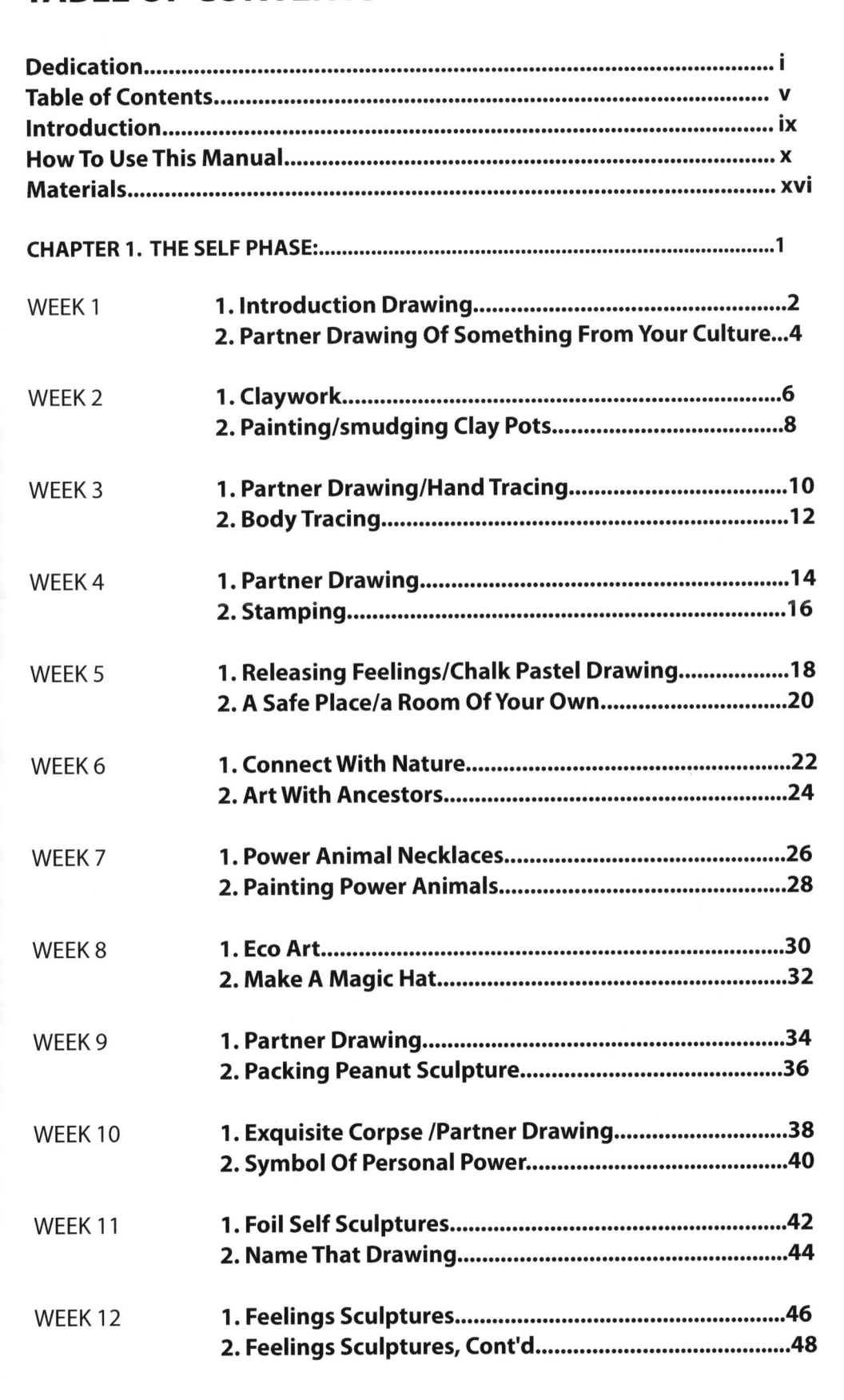

TABLE OF CONTENTS

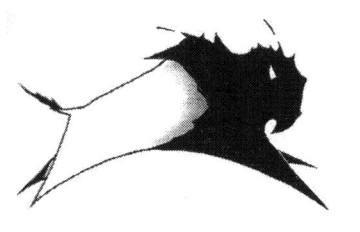

Dedication.. i	
Table of Contents.. v	
Introduction... ix	
How To Use This Manual.. x	
Materials... xvi	

CHAPTER 1. THE SELF PHASE:..1

WEEK 1	1. Introduction Drawing..2
	2. Partner Drawing Of Something From Your Culture...4

WEEK 2	1. Claywork..6
	2. Painting/smudging Clay Pots....................................8

WEEK 3	1. Partner Drawing/Hand Tracing................................10
	2. Body Tracing..12

WEEK 4	1. Partner Drawing..14
	2. Stamping...16

WEEK 5	1. Releasing Feelings/Chalk Pastel Drawing................18
	2. A Safe Place/a Room Of Your Own.........................20

WEEK 6	1. Connect With Nature...22
	2. Art With Ancestors..24

WEEK 7	1. Power Animal Necklaces...26
	2. Painting Power Animals..28

WEEK 8	1. Eco Art..30
	2. Make A Magic Hat..32

WEEK 9	1. Partner Drawing..34
	2. Packing Peanut Sculpture..36

WEEK 10	1. Exquisite Corpse /Partner Drawing.........................38
	2. Symbol Of Personal Power......................................40

WEEK 11	1. Foil Self Sculptures..42
	2. Name That Drawing..44

WEEK 12	1. Feelings Sculptures..46
	2. Feelings Sculptures, Cont'd.....................................48

TABLE OF CONTENTS

CHAPTER 2. THE PROBLEM PHASE: 51

WEEK 1
1. Introduction Collages 52
2. Magic Carpet Ride 54

WEEK 2
1. Treasure Box Delivery 56
2. Seeing Your Future 58

WEEK 3
1. Who Are You? 60
2. Leader Or Bully? 62

WEEK 4
1. Draw A Bridge 64
2. Draw Your Initials 66

WEEK 5
1. The Best/Worst Thing I Could Be 68
2. Acting In A Feeling /Acting Out A Feeling 70

WEEK 6
1. Anger Collage 72
2. Anger Boxes 74

WEEK 7
1. When I Am Stressed/ Not Stressed 76
2. Partner Sculpture 78

WEEK 8
1. Prayer Flags 80
2. When I Am Anxious/ When I Am Not Anxious 82

WEEK 9
1. Coping Wheel 84
2. Kindness Toward Others 86

WEEK 10
1. Rocket Ship 88
2. Friendship 90

WEEK 11
1. Giving To The World 92
2. Collage Of Feelings 94

WEEK 12
1. Solve A Problem 96
2. Draw Yourself In Your Favorite Season 98

TABLE OF CONTENTS

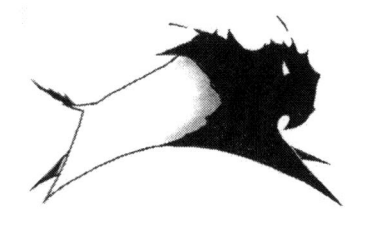

CHAPTER 3. THE TRANSFORMATION PHASE: 101

WEEK 1
1. Container Of Tools 102
2. Design Your Own Book Cover 104

WEEK 2
1. Make An Advertisement For Yourself 106
2. Draw A Bridge 108

WEEK 3
1. Family Of Animals 110
2. Family Of Animals, Continued 112

WEEK 4
1. Family Of Animals, Continued 114
2. Positive Coping Skills 116

WEEK 5
1. Negative Coping Skills 118
2. Classroom Problem / Solution 120

WEEK 6
1. Thankful To Our Ancestors 122
2. Complete A Picture 124

WEEK 7
1. Someone You Admire 126
2. The Ugliest Drawing 128

WEEK 8
1. Honor Your Past/Future 130
2. Honoring Your Ancestors/elders 132

CHAPTER 4. THE INTEGRATION PHASE: 135

WEEK 1
1. Collage Of Support System 136
2. My World 138

WEEK 2
1. Boundary Bowls 140
2. Boundary Bowls, Continued 142

WEEK 3
1. Create A Rainbow 144
2. Mandalas 146

WEEK 4
1. Response Art 148
2. Response Art, Continued 150

Conclusion 153
References 154

Introduction

Start Up!© is a year-long school-based arts intervention classroom curriculum was developed by Art Therapist, Linda Chapman, MA, ATR-BC and Carey MacCarthy, MA, ATR-LPCC, an Art Therapist and Licensed Professional Clinical Counselor. The Start Up! curriculum was formulated to help heal indigenous children and children of all ethnicities within a classroom environement. The Start Up! Curriculum was culturally modified by Carey MacCarthy with guidance from Native American Cultural Advisors from the Lakota Tribe in South Dakota.

This curriculum utilizes Linda Chapman's Neurodevelopmental Art Therapy (NDAT) four stage evidence-based chronic trauma treatment model designed to strengthen neural pathways for organic impairments, reducing anxiety, depression and aggression, and treat ADD/ADHD, PTSD, substance abuse, violent behavior and suicide. This evidence-based model also has the ability to increase classroom attention span, participation and test scores. We have made this trauma treatment model culturally competent and culturally relevant to the Native American population and all cultures in order to provide holistic healing for the whole child within their own cultural heritage.

Note: The Start Up! program can be adapted to any culture or ethnicity. Please ensure that cultural adaptation of the curriculum maintains, cultural neutrality : that it is neutral, and respects all beliefs and values within the given culture. Example: When working with the Native American culture, we would not suggest asking children to draw the Native American Sacred Pipe, as many children's families have different spiritual/religious beliefs and values. You may ask the children, "Draw something that is important to you from your culture." In this way, you are not introducing nor imposing potentially controversial topics onto the children, which may cause family discomfort.

Neurodevelopmental Art Therapy for Trauma Treatment and Developmental Issues

Research has proven that trauma is stored in the right brain. Art is a right brain activity with the power to access traumatic memories and bodily based sensations stored in the right brain. When a child or youth is exposed to trauma for a long period of time, the right brain is constantly activated, resulting in left brain inactivity (Perry, 1005). The left brain is the location of new learning and memory retention. When the left brain begins to atrophy, a child cannot learn in school, resulting in low test scores, low IQ's, low self-esteem, and high drop-out rates. Language is a left brain activity. When children speak about their art, the left brain is engaged along with the right hemisphere activation via the art making. Art Therapy activates both sides of the brain, creating a clear channel of communication between the hemispheres, and allowing the forming, strengthening or re-wiring of neural pathways.

When the brain is functioning optimally, the child will exhibit more abilities in: emotional stability, coordination of both sides of body, mature motor planning (movement), balance, visual perception, language, body awareness, and eye-hand coordination. We will also see a reduction in anxiety, stress, fear, depression, oppositional defiance, and aggression. In the child we will also see an increase in: trust, attention span, concentration, memory, ability to self-soothe, planning, judgment, empathy, compassion, wisdom, understanding consequences, an increase in test scores, IQ's, and c lassroom attendance.

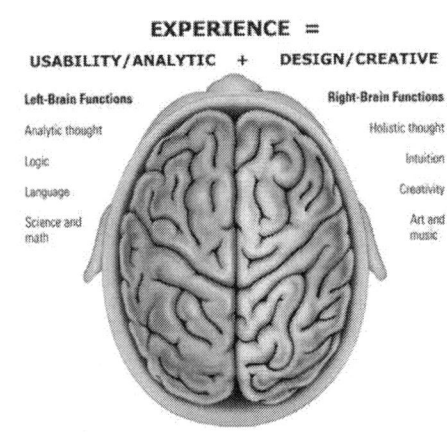

Tony Buzan, Exercise Your Creativity-Mind Mapping. Amaya Thinking, April 2008.

The Start Up! Curriculum: How To Use This Manual

This curriculum is designed for K-12, for both children and adolescents alike. Adolescents appreciate the opportunity to revisit childhood activities: it is enjoyable and fun for ALL ages (even adults enjoy it!). By closely following the Start Up! arts intervention curriculum, you will begin to see positive changes in the children and adolescents.

This Facilitator's Manual is divided into Four Sections for a clearly outlined weekly approach to each session. Any section can be repeated as needed before moving onto the next section. Repetition of these activities is beneficial and encouraged, as it reinforces the creation or strengthening of neural pathways, and creates safety as the child knows what to expect when repeating an exercise.

DURATION	PHASE	GOALS / ARTS
12 WEEKS	SELF PHASE	**PHYSICAL HOMEOSTASIS** Identity Formation/Sensory Motor Development
12 WEEKS	PROBLEM PHASE	**EMOTIONAL HOMEOSTASIS** Exploration of Feelings & Perception
8 WEEKS	TRANSFORMATION PHASE	**COGNITIVE HOMEOSTASIS** Understanding past / present & reclaiming self
4 WEEKS	INTEGRATION PHASE	**CREATIVITY** Identifying support & future orientation

It is important and advantageous to follow the Start Up! Curriculum in the order presented. Understand that all 4 phases within the Start Up! program are a part of a continuum, and need to be completed from beginning to end for optimum results.

Note: Not following the Start Up! curriculum order may minimize the effectiveness of the program. It is strongly recommended you follow the phases in the suggested order until completed.

Although the art activities are therapeutic they are specifically designed not to be Art Therapy or Art Psychotherapy. The art directives to strengthen sensory and motor systems develop the mind-body self and allow children to discover new possibilities for their lives and their future.

The Start Up! Curriculum: How To Use This Manual

For optimal benefit, we recommend offering this curriculum to your classroom twice per week, on Thursday or Friday and again on Monday. The reason for this is many children live in or around traumatic environments. By engaging them in art activities, which specifically provides a coping skill, before children return home to these traumatic environments, and again on Monday, providing "feelings release" art, after they have returned from potential traumatic experiences, will significantly reduce long-term effects of any new traumas.

MONDAY- Start Up! Session to provide "feelings release" from emotion they are holding from potential exposure to traumatic events from previous weekend.

FRIDAY- Start Up! Session to provide coping skills to prepare the child for re-entering potentially traumatic environments or experiencing traumatic events during weekend.

Grade K-12 will have varying abilities and attention spans according to age and developmental levels. You can use the graph below to determine the duration of your Start Up! Sessions. You may increase or decrease durations accordingly.

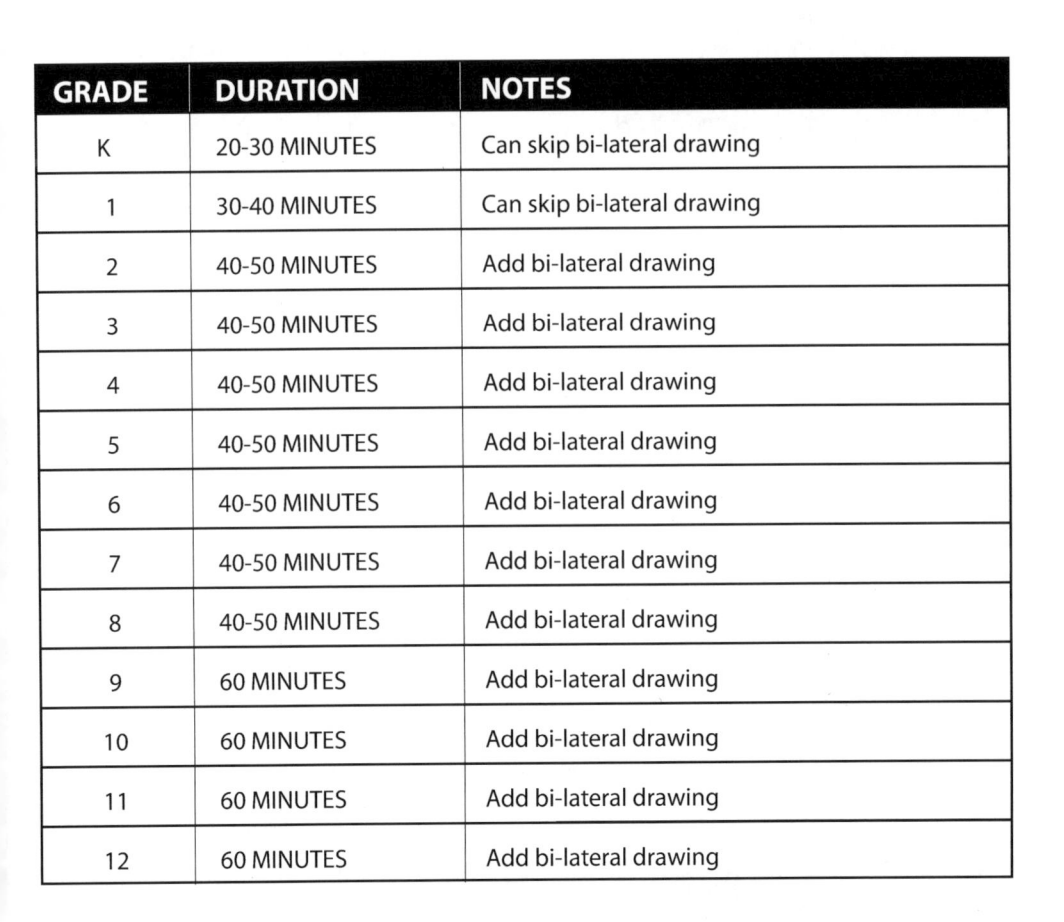

GRADE	DURATION	NOTES
K	20-30 MINUTES	Can skip bi-lateral drawing
1	30-40 MINUTES	Can skip bi-lateral drawing
2	40-50 MINUTES	Add bi-lateral drawing
3	40-50 MINUTES	Add bi-lateral drawing
4	40-50 MINUTES	Add bi-lateral drawing
5	40-50 MINUTES	Add bi-lateral drawing
6	40-50 MINUTES	Add bi-lateral drawing
7	40-50 MINUTES	Add bi-lateral drawing
8	40-50 MINUTES	Add bi-lateral drawing
9	60 MINUTES	Add bi-lateral drawing
10	60 MINUTES	Add bi-lateral drawing
11	60 MINUTES	Add bi-lateral drawing
12	60 MINUTES	Add bi-lateral drawing

NOTE: It is recommended to participate in a Start Up! training to more fully comprehend the neurobiology of trauma and the benefits of Art Therapy. For training information please visit www.indigenoushealingarts.org or call 415-947-9608

Purpose & Benefits

The Purpose & Benefits is located at the left-hand margin of every Start Up! session. This column includes a brief phase description of each of the four phases of the Start Up! curriculum, and how each art session correlates to specific neural activity in the healing of trauma. Also included in the Purpose & Benefits column is a list of developmental goals, which are developed and improved as a result of each activity.

Glossary of Terms

Self Expression- The ability to communicate verbally and non-verbally.
Community Building- The ability to strengthen relationships among peers and others.
Celebrating Uniqueness/Diversity- Developing acceptance for differences.
Creating Trust- Providing a sense of safety, comfort, and ease of participation.
Creating Safety- Providing adequate supervision and support for the child to grow and develop.
Perceptual Development- The process of taking in and organizing sensory information from the environment.
Building Self-Esteem- Reinforcing and developing a positive mind-body concept of Self.
Identity Formation- Development of a positive mind-body concept of Self.
Development of Abstract Thinking- The ability to think about concepts that are not factual.
Eye-hand Coordination- The ability for the brain to communicate to the body, a preferred course of action.
Experience of Control- The ability to manage one's behavior and emotions.
Decision Making- The ability to take in information, consider consequences and make meaningful choices.
Development of Imagination- The ability to imagine new concepts that are not factual.
Emotional Development- The ability to identify and regulate feelings.
Opportunity for Choices- The ability to think independently and make choices based on one's perceptions.
Promotes Critical Thinking- The evaluation of information to form a judgment.
Emotional Regulation- The ability to identify and respond to feelings in a socially appropriate way.
Development of Social Skills- The ability to adapt within established social norms and rules for positive social interaction.
Installation of Hope- To foster support and broaden the cultivation of new possibilities.
Acknowledging the Past- The ability to identify and understand one's personal and cultural history.

Terms can be found in the Purpose and Benefits section.

Purpose & Benefits

Cultivating Cultural Pride/Identity- Developing an awareness and affinity for one's ancestral heritage and cultural traditions.

Tactile Discrimination- The ability to differentiate various physical sensations through the sense of touch (wet/dry, rough/smooth).

Visual/Spatial Organization- The ability to interpret what the eyes see (distance between objects, location of object in space), essential for mathematical proficiency.

Building Self Concept- Reinforcing positive beliefs one holds about oneself.

Self Identity- Recognition of one's qualities as an individual.

Exploring Preferences- The ability to identify and express one's wants and needs.

Broaden Repertoire of Intellectual Concepts- To stimulate and enhance curiosity.

Future Orientation- The ability to plan and implement a series of steps to achieve a goal.

Delaying Gratification- The ability to put off something now, in order to attain something greater in the future.

Patience- The capacity to accept or tolerate a range of emotions without responding negatively.

Normalize Emotions- To universalize common experiences and feelings shared by others.

Transforming Negative to Positive- Reframing or providing a wider context about an issue or behavior to alter maladaptive behaviors to socially acceptable ones.

Increases Problem Solving Abilities- The ability to identify a problem and devise a menu of choices for solving the problem.

Development of Aesthetics- The development of appreciation for color, composition, form and beauty.

Emotional Recognition- To identify and define a feeling state.

Emotional Containment- The ability to tolerate and regulate a wide variety of emotional stimuli.

Define/Describe Loss- Examining feelings of loss due to loss of somebody or functioning that results in a state of grief.

Expressing Wants/Needs- The ability to identify and communicate one's emotional and physical wants/needs to others in an appropriate manner.

Learning Adaptive Coping Strategies- To learn pro-social, adaptive methods for positively managing emotions and behavior.

Prevention- To hinder or decrease maladaptive behaviors for coping and managing stress.

Developing Altruism- To develop the capacity to demonstrate care and concern for the well-being of others.

Identifying/Expressing Positive Emotions- The ability to identify and express positive feelings for self and others.

Self Disclosure- The ability to share information about one's self in a socially appropriate manner.

Terms can be found in the Purpose and Benefits section.

Start Up! Sessions

Start with a brief explanation of the time allotted for the activity. Remind children halfway through the session time, and again, remind them at the last 5 minutes that the activity will be wrapping up and that they will have time to share at the end.

Each Start Up! session consists of 6 key elements:

- Movement/Sound
- Breathing/Meditation
- Bi-lateral Scribble
- Bi-lateral Drawing
- Art Activity
- Closure/Discussion

Each element plays an important role in the neurobiological healing of trauma in the Start Up! curriculum, therefore it is important to complete each element within each session of the Start Up! curriculum. If you are working with younger children who find it very challenging to do the bi-lateral drawing, you can move onto the art activity directly after the bi-lateral scribble. If your time is tight, it is okay to shorten the time given to the each of the elements. Below you will find an explanation of each element.

Movement/ Sound (3 minutes)
Simon Says/Head, Shoulders, Knees and Toes/ Music Freeze (Auditory/Kinesthetic stimulation [hearing/ body] & Auditory processing- sensory activity, which helps to activate the cerebellum.) Children may keep moving due to lack of impulse control. Begin activities with one of these to activate the lower part of the brain.

Breathing / Meditation (3-5 minutes)
It is proven that 3 breaths physiologically relaxes the body. You can do this whenever a child is stressed or when the class needs calming. Include this before the art activity. You can work up to breathing for 2, 3, or 5 minutes. Instruct the children sit up straight, to close their eyes, and breathe in and out slowly through their nose (unless they have a stuffy nose). Have the class begin with breathing every time before the bi-lateral scribble.

Bi-Lateral Scribble (3 minutes)
This very effective technique engages both sides of the brain, incorporating drawing on both sides of the body, tactile stimulation (sense of touch) and auditory processing (sense of hearing). Children become calm and alert.

Start Up! Sessions

Bi-Lateral Drawing (3 minutes)
Similar to bi-lateral scribble, that it engages the tactile and auditory senses as children are drawing with both sides of the body and having to listen to directions, AND also adds the additional challenge of trying to draw with both hands at the same time- very fun! The facilitator can include cultural teachings: "Draw the Plains, tipis and buffalo, or draw a tropical rainforest and monkeys, or draw the ocean and some whales." This can be tailored to the environment the children's ethnicity is originated from and include oral tradition with historical stories and cultural teachings.

Art Activity (see graph for time duration- time your session accordingly)
The art activities in the Start Up! curriculum are specifically designed to engage certain areas of the brain to aid in the creation, strengthening and re-wiring of neural activity, as well as to form personal and cultural identity, explore problems, create boundaries, instill a sense of safety and hope, develop coping strategies and self-esteem, and build community. Each art activity is culturally neutral and culturally competent.

Closure/Discussion (10-15 minutes)
This element provides the left brain verbal expression important in conjunction with the right brain art activity, which helps both brain hemispheres to communicate. The closure/discussion also builds peer relations and understanding of the self.

All of the following activities are designed to be done in a classroom and can also be done in individual sessions with a teacher or therapist. The adult time and attention will keep the child engaged in the activity and, importantly, safety must be a primary concern. Some activities require more adult supervision than others. Some activities will provide other positive sensory experiences in another category, as the activities are only listed once. When the child is no longer having fun, delay the activity or pick another activity.

Pre- School/Kindergarten Adaptation
When working with younger children who are just learning how to do small tasks such as tear tape and remove pen caps, etc., it is important to help them feel successful. Facilitating Start Up! in small groups of 4-5 is best. During the bi-lateral scribble activity, it may be difficult for the younger children to tear tape and tape their paper onto their desk, or to remember to use both hands while doing the scribble. Perhaps the teacher has the paper taped to the table when the children come in to the classroom first thing in the morning, or after recess. Some children will move both pens to one hand out of habit. Gently reminding them to use two hands while scribbling is important. We advise that children receive help and learn how to do these tasks as they will eventually be able to do it on their own, therefore small groups will help the children immensely.

You may choose to omit the "bi-lateral drawing" as it may prove to be more difficult until children are in the first or second grade. Some may be able to draw objects with both hands, whereas others may not be able to.

Materials Needed

- Markers
- Crayons
- Colored Pencils
- Oil Pastels
- Chalk Pastels
- Model Magic Air Dry Clay (Crayola)
- Plaster Gauze
- Recycled Materials: (tea /toothpaste/cereal/butter boxes, wood, coffee cans, soda bottles, fabric, buttons, ribbon, etc- ask families to save from home)
- Cardboard Boxes
- Acrylic Paints (Red, Blue, Yellow, Brown, Black, White- children encouraged to mix colors themselves)
- Watercolor Paint (in trays)
- Golden Taklon Brushes (Different sizes)
- Painters Tape
- Masking Tape
- Glue Sticks
- School Glue
- Scissors
- Drawing Paper (9x13 or 11x17.)
- Watercolor Paper (9x13 or 11x17.)
- Large Butcher/Art Paper (White/colored)
- Construction Paper
- Magazines for collage
- Tissue Paper, assorted colors
- Foil
- Toothpicks

THE SELF PHASE - 12 weeks

The following activities are designed to offer children safe and enjoyable experiences that will promote development.

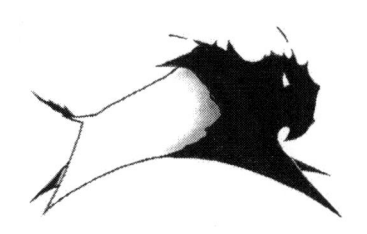

Objective

This 12 week segment will focus on sensory art, which corresponds with the lower functioning level of the brain called the cerebellum. Sensory Art stimulates the 5 senses: sight, sound, touch, smell, taste. Sensory-motor functions regulate the input, organization, and output of information. Delays in sensory-motor functioning can be very small and still cause problems in the following areas:

- Emotional stability
- Coordination of both sides of body
- Mature motor planning (movement)
- Balance
- Visual perception
- Language
- Body awareness
- Eye-hand coordination

By stimulating the lowest part of the brain (cerebellum) using sensory motor art, the right hemisphere of the brain is engaged, followed by higher levels of brain activity, moving from lower structures to higher structures. This, along with increased cooperation between hemispheres allows for cortical consolidation and integration of trauma. This is demonstrated in the experience being in explicit memory, or accessible via language.

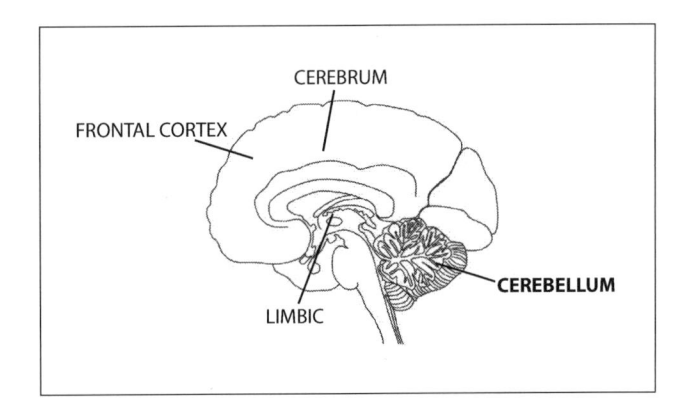

WEEK 1

INTRODUCTION DRAWING

SELF PHASE

Purpose:
Physical Homeostasis

Goal:
Identity Formation/
Sensory Motor
Development

Neural Activity:
Cerebellum

Benefits:
- Self expression/ disclosure
- Community Building
- Celebrating Uniqueness/ Diversity
- Creating Trust
- Experience of Control

Duration:
12 Weeks

Session 1 - Monday

ACTIVITY: INTRODUCTION DRAWING

Art Materials:
- Markers
- Oil Pastels
- Largest paper for the desk space
- 3 Pieces each of 9 x 12 paper
- Painters tape

SIMON SAYS

BREATHING / MEDITATION
"Close your eyes or leave them open if you would like. Breathe in deeply through your nose or mouth, until your lungs are full. Let your breath out until your lungs are empty." Do this 3 times, or as many times as you are able. You can set a timer for longer and longer times, up to 3-5 minutes.

ART DIRECTIVES:
A. Bi-Lateral Scribble:
Two handed Marker drawing (1 Marker/crayon for each hand): Each movement is done for 9-10 seconds. We encourage the children to look at their marks on the paper, the teacher can stand at the front of the group and demonstrate on the chalkboard, describing the process of bilateral scribbling **(Younger children may need help with taping and movements at first):**
1. Tape Paper onto table (horizontally).
2. Make Random Marks with both hands.
3. Make Vertical Lines beginning from the bottom of the paper to the top, up and down. (can alternate hands).
4. Make Horizontal Lines, across paper with each hand on opposite edge of page," bringing their markers to meet in the middle. Have children cross the midline (cross arms to opposite sides of the paper and back to opposite side of page-repeat)
5. Make two Arcs, or windshield wiper movements, back and forth. Let the Arcs move into two large circles and go around and around.
6. Continue to make Circles in the reverse direction,- reverse again/ repeating.
7. Make gentle Dots- now go up and down on the paper, now back and forth across the paper.
8. Put one arm and hand over the other and make a Big X and now move the other arm and hand on top, now the other on top (repeat 4-5 times)
9. Make Fast Circles, go around really fast, now gradually slower and smaller, until you have a small circle add dot in the middle of the smallest circle, and STOP.

Start Up! Facilitator Manual

INTRODUCTION DRAWING

WEEK 1

B. Bi-Lateral Drawing:
Flip paper and re-tape paper to table
With markers in each hand children are instructed to:
1. Draw a groundline
2. Draw a house with windows and door (tipi, wigwam, hut, traditional home, can add cultural teachings about traditional homes of particular population)
3. Draw a tree
4. Draw a basket of apples underneath the tree (or can be traditional food and add cultural teachings about the traditional foods of particular population)
5. Put clouds up in the sky
6. Sun / Birds

MOTIVATION: "This is a good way to introduce each other and the Start Up! art program to the class. "We are all unique individuals with different interests. Today we get to introduce ourselves through our drawings. Please do not laugh or judge each other's work. This is a safe place to share without judgement."

C. Introduction Drawing:
1. Child folds paper in half.
2. On outside of paper child draws introduction drawing of what they would like us to know about themselves.
3. On the inside of folded paper child draws what others may not know about them.
   Teacher: Emphasize how each child is different and special. That no person is better than the other, that we all have our own gifts and talents and how important is to accept and honor each child, to never call them names or bully them for their special differences.
4. Have children share their images. Children do not have to share if they do not want, and do not have to share what they don't want us to know about themselves.

CLOSURE/ DISCUSSION:

- What do you like best about yourself?

- What did you notice or learn about yourself today?

Facilitator Manual — Start Up!

WEEK 1

USING BOTH SIDES OF THE BODY/PARTNER DRAWING OF SOMETHING FROM YOUR CULTURE

SELF PHASE

Purpose:
Physical Homeostasis

Goal:
Identity Formation/
Sensory Motor
Development

Neural Activity:
Cerebellum

Benefits:
- Community Building
- Cultural Identity
- Creating Trust

Duration:
12 Weeks

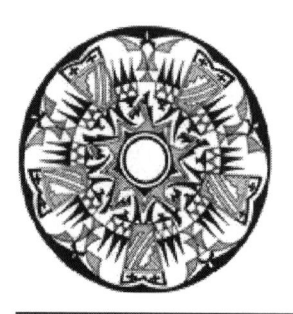

Session 2 - Friday

ACTIVITY: USING BOTH SIDES OF THE BODY/PARTNER DRAWING OF SOMETHING FROM YOUR CULTURE

Art Materials:
- Markers,
- Largest paper for the desk space
- 3 Pieces each of 9 x 12 paper

HEAD/SHOULDER/KNEES & TOES

BREATHING / MEDITATION
"Close your eyes or leave them open if you would like. Breathe in deeply through your nose or mouth, until your lungs are full. Let your breath out until your lungs are empty. Sit comfortably, feel your feet on the ground. Breathe in and imagine a white light filling your body. Let it out. Imagine a color that represents your stress. Where in your body is this stress color? Breathe in the white light and let it take over your stress. Breathe out the stress color. Breathe in white light into your entire body, from your toes to the top of your head." You can set a timer for longer and longer times, up to 3-5 minutes.

ART DIRECTIVES:
A. Bi-Lateral Scribble:
   Two handed Marker drawing (1 Marker/crayon for each hand):
Each movement is done for 9-10 seconds. We encourage the children to look at their marks on the paper, the teacher can stand at the front of the group and demonstrate on the chalkboard, describing the process of bilateral scribbling **(Younger children may need help with taping and movements at first):**
   1. Tape Paper onto table (horizontally).
   2. Make Random Marks with both hands.
   3. Make Vertical Lines beginning from the bottom of the paper to the top, up and down. (can alternate hands).
   4. Make Horizontal Lines, across paper with each hand on opposite edge of page," bringing their markers to meet in the middle. Have children cross the midline (cross arms to opposite sides of the paper and back to opposite side of page-repeat)
   5. Make two Arcs, or windshield wiper movements, back and forth. Let the Arcs move into two large circles and go around and around.
   6. Continue to make Circles in the reverse direction,- reverse again/ repeating.
   7. Make gentle Dots- now go up and down on the paper, now back and forth across the paper.

4   Start Up!   Facilitator Manual

USING BOTH SIDES OF THE BODY/PARTNER DRAWING OF SOMETHING FROM YOUR CULTURE

WEEK 1

A. Bi-Lateral Scribble Cont.:
8. Put one arm and hand over the other and make a Big X and now move the other arm and hand on top, now the other on top (repeat 4-5 times)
9. Make Fast Circles, go around really fast, now gradually slower and smaller, until you have a small circle add dot in the middle of the smallest circle, and STOP.

B. Bi-Lateral Drawing:
Flip paper and re-tape paper to table
With markers in each hand children are instructed to:
1. Draw a starry sky
2. Draw some star people (can add cultural teachings about traditional star knowledge beliefs of particular population)
3. Draw a spaceship
4. Draw a moon

C. Scribble Chase
1. Select a partner (each child has 1 marker)
2. Determine who will be the leader, the follower
3. Say "GO" and the leader leads with the marker and the follower tries to follow the leader on the paper with their marker (30-40 seconds each turn)
4. Switch roles

MOTIVATION: "We are going to have fun today…We are going to use both sides of the body to draw. What happens when you draw with your non-dominant hand? It gets both sides of the brain activated and communicating."

D. Partner Drawings (with same partner)
1. Think about something from your culture- could be a traditional home, or an animal or a ceremony or object that are specific to your culture.
2. Tell your partner what it is you are thinking of.
3. On Shared Piece of Paper, one child makes a mark to start drawing the object, animal, etc from their culture and returns paper to other child to make a different mark on the paper who is drawing the same thing. (Try making marks with other hand)
4. Continue exchanging drawings for 1-2 minutes.
5. Flip the paper over and the other child leads the process on the new paper.
6. *Teacher:* **Emphasize the partnership and the feeling that someone is there for them and how important it is to remember this feeling whenever child is lonely, sad, scared, etc.**

CLOSURE/ DISCUSSION:

- What activity did you like best, least?
- Which did you like best being the leader or the follower?
- What was it like to do the partner drawings?
- Having friends are important because?
- Whenever you feel sad, mad, etc you can think about a friend or tell a friend and feel better.
- What did you notice or learn about yourself today?
- What did you learn about the kind of friend you can be?

WEEK 2

USING BOTH SIDES OF THE BODY/CLAYWORK

SELF PHASE

Purpose:
Physical Homeostasis

Goal:
Identity Formation/
Sensory Motor
Development

Neural Activity:
Cerebellum

Benefits:
• Emotional
  Regulation
• Emotional
  Recognition
• Emotional
  Containment
• Eye-hand
  Coordination
• Learning adaptive
  coping strategies

Duration:
12 Weeks

Session 1 - Monday

ACTIVITY: USING BOTH SIDES OF THE BODY/CLAYWORK

Art Materials:
• Markers
• Largest paper for the desk space
• Model Magic Clay- 1oz bag per 2 children

MUSIC FREEZE

BREATHING / MEDITATION
"Breathe deeply, in and out slowly. Imagine yourself back as early as you can remember. Imagine seeing yourself in the mirror, back when you had baby teeth. What did your face look like? What did your hair look like? Look at your hands and feet, see how small they were. Take a moment to be thankful for your health at that age. Now imagine yourself a little older. What does your face look like in the mirror now? What do your teeth look like now? How are you wearing your hair? What is your favorite shirt? What are your favorite pants? Look at your hands and feet. Think about how it felt to be this age. Take a moment to be thankful for your health at this age. Now imagine you are the age you are now and you are looking in the mirror. See yourself how you are now. Appreciate and admire yourself. We all are different, and we are all unique. Appreciate your differences, and know that you are beautiful just the way you are. Take a moment to be thankful for your health at this age. Imagine yourself when you are an adult. Imagine how you might wear your hair. Imagine if you might have a beard, moustache, if you're a man (girls might want to grow a beard or moustache or draw one on, this is ok), how you might wear your make-up as a girl (if you're a man you might wish to wear make-up too, this is ok). What kind of clothes will you wear? What kind of job will you have? Will you a have a family of your own? Honor your body for the abilities you have."

ART DIRECTIVES:
A. Bi-Lateral Scribble:
   Two handed Marker drawing (1 Marker/crayon for each hand):
Each movement is done for 9-10 seconds. We encourage the children to look at their marks on the paper, the teacher can stand at the front of the group and demonstrate on the chalkboard, describing the process of bilateral scribbling **(Younger children may need help with taping and movements at first):**
   1. Tape Paper onto table (horizontally).
   2. Make Random Marks with both hands.
   3. Make Vertical Lines beginning from the bottom of the paper to the top, up and down. (can alternate hands).
   4. Make Horizontal Lines, across paper with each hand on opposite edge of page," bringing their markers to meet in the middle. Have children cross the midline (cross arms to opposite sides of the paper and back to opposite side of page-repeat)
   5. Make two Arcs, or windshield wiper movements, back and forth.
      Let the Arcs move into two large circles and go around and around.

Start Up! Facilitator Manual

USING BOTH SIDES OF THE BODY/CLAYWORK — WEEK 2

A. Bi-Lateral Scribble Cont.:
6. Continue to make Circles in the reverse direction,- reverse again/repeating.
7. Make gentle Dots- now go up and down on the paper, now back and forth across the paper.
8. Put one arm and hand over the other and make a Big X and now move the other arm and hand on top, now the other on top (repeat 4-5 times)
9. Make Fast Circles, go around really fast, now gradually slower and smaller, until you have a small circle add dot in the middle of the smallest circle, and STOP.

B. Bi-Lateral Drawing:
Flip paper and re-tape paper to table
With markers in each hand children are instructed to:
1. Draw a waterline
2. Draw a boat (can be a traditional boat of particular population and add cultural teachings)
3. Draw a motor or sails to the boat (if applicable)
4. Draw a flag
5. Draw someone fishing with a line in the water with a hook
6. Draw some fish in the water
7. Add a shark
8. Draw a starfish in the water
9. Add clouds/sun/birds
10. TEACHER- If you are a people originated near water, include cultural traditions and stories of water.

MOTIVATION: "Who knows what a bowl is for? It can hold any feelings you want to get out of your body. Think about a feeling you would like to release and put it into the clay as you are making your bowl. This is what we are going to do today."

C. Clay Work (half pkg per child)- Releasing Feelings into Clay
1. Everyone roll clay into ball
2. Smash the ball flat
3. Roll into another ball
4. Roll into a long snake
5. Roll into ball and pound flat
6. Roll into ball again
7. Pinch Pot- insert thumbs into ball and squeeze along edges until a bowl is formed.
8. Smash pot into ball
9. Make coil pot- take a small piece of clay, roll into ball and flatten it.
10. Make a snake with the other piece and coil it onto flattened ball.
11. Make any pot you would like to make
12. Air Dry
13. *Teacher:* **Remind child to release any feelings into the clay. (Make extra pots for absent children so they will have something to paint next session.) Smudge pots with sage, copal, etc.**

CLOSURE/DISCUSSION:

- Which pot did you like to make best? Were you able to release your feelings?

- Do you feel better? How did it feel to smudge your pot?

OR

- Pots are made to give and receive things, what would you like to give or receive with your pot?

Facilitator Manual — Start Up!

WEEK 2

PAINTING/SMUDGING CLAY POTS

SELF PHASE

Purpose:
Physical Homeostasis

Goal:
Identity Formation/
Sensory Motor
Development

Neural Activity:
Cerebellum

Benefits:
- Perceptual Development
- Emotional Regulation
- Emotional Recognition
- Emotional Containment
- Eye-hand Coordination
- Learning adaptive coping strategies
- Delaying gratification
- Patience

Duration:
12 Weeks

Session 2 - Friday

ACTIVITY: PAINTING/SMUDGING CLAY POTS

Art Materials:
- Markers
- Largest paper for the desk space
- Small bowls of different colored paint at each table
- Different sized paint brushes
- Clay pots made by children the week before. (Have extras ready for children who were absent.)
- Bowl of purifying herbs to burn- Sage, copal, tea leaves, palo santo, etc

SIMON SAYS

BREATHING / MEDITATION
"Breathe deeply, in and out slowly. Imagine you have grown up and you are a world famous dancer. Imagine what it would feel like to be on stage in front of many people applauding for you. What would your costume/regalia look like? What kind of music would you dance to? Would you dance to traditional music from your culture or modern, or another's culture?"

ART DIRECTIVES:
A. Bi-Lateral Scribble:
   Two handed Marker drawing (1 Marker/crayon for each hand):
Each movement is done for 9-10 seconds. We encourage the children to look at their marks on the paper, the teacher can stand at the front of the group and demonstrate on the chalkboard, describing the process of bilateral scribbling **(Younger children may need help with taping and movements at first):**
  1. Tape Paper onto table (horizontally).
  2. Make Random Marks with both hands.
  3. Make Vertical Lines beginning from the bottom of the paper to the top, up and down. (can alternate hands).
  4. Make Horizontal Lines, across paper with each hand on opposite edge of page," bringing their markers to meet in the middle. Have children cross the midline (cross arms to opposite sides of the paper and back to opposite side of page-repeat)
  5. Make two Arcs, or windshield wiper movements, back and forth. Let the Arcs move into two large circles and go around and around.
  6. Continue to make Circles in the reverse direction,- reverse again/repeating.

Start Up! Facilitator Manual

PAINTING/SMUDGING CLAY POTS

WEEK 2

A. Bi-Lateral Scribble Cont.:
7. Make gentle Dots- now go up and down on the paper, now back and forth across the paper.
8. Put one arm and hand over the other and make a Big X and now move the other arm and hand on top, now the other on top (repeat 4-5 times)
9. Make Fast Circles, go around really fast, now gradually slower and smaller, until you have a small circle add dot in the middle of the smallest circle, and STOP.

B. Bi-Lateral Drawing:
Flip paper and re-tape paper to table.
With markers in each hand children are instructed to:
1. Draw underground
2. Draw a snake underground
3. Draw a family of snakes underground
4. Draw a prairie dog underground
5. Draw a fox
6. Draw a rabbit
7. Add a family of rabbits
8. Draw some ants
9. Add clouds/sun/birds above ground

MOTIVATION: "Remember the pots we made last week? Today we are going to paint them. These are going to be our very own special bowls and you can paint them any way you like. Can anyone tell me what color they would like to paint their bowl?"

C. Painting Clay Pots
1. Have different traditional ceramic designs shown on chalk board
2. Give smaller children a lesson on dipping brush in paint and wiping excess off (cleaning brush in water before changing color, etc)
3. Demonstrate different painting techniques (lines, dots, crooked lines, stripes)
4. Include traditional teachings on indigenous uses of clay pots; for holding water, cooking. Describe how pots were made from clay in nature, and traditional firing techniques while children are painting.
5. Can play soft traditional music in background
6. ***Teachers:* Smudge pots with sage, copal, palo santo, sweet grass, tea leaves, etc, and say a prayer for all the feelings to be taken out of the pots and transformed into healing for the children.**

CLOSURE/DISCUSSION:

- What color did you paint your bowl and why?

- Was it easy or hard to paint your bowl?

- What do you think you will put in your bowl?

- How do you feel now that your feelings are out of your body and have been smudged away by the sage, copal, palo santo, etc?

- If you feel any bad feelings this weekend, know that you can remember what it felt like to release your feelings into the clay and smudge them away.

Facilitator Manual   Start Up!   9

WEEK 3

USING BOTH SIDES OF THE BODY/ PARTNER DRAWING, HAND TRACING

SELF PHASE

Purpose:
Physical Homeostasis

Goal:
Identity Formation/ Sensory Motor Development

Neural Activity:
Cerebellum

Benefits:
- Perceptual Development
- Community Building
- Listening to Directions- Auditory Stimulation
- Celebrating Diversity/Teaching Acceptance

Duration:
12 Weeks

Session 1 - Monday

ACTIVITY: USING BOTH SIDES OF THE BODY/PARTNER DRAWING, HAND TRACING

Art Materials:
- Markers
- Pastel (Oil/Chalk)
- Largest paper for the desk space
- 3 Pieces each of 9x12 paper
- 1 Piece of Butcher Paper (lg enough to glue all hands on in a circle)
- Glue

HEAD SHOULDERS KNEES AND TOES

BREATHING / MEDITATION
"Breathe deeply, in and out slowly. Sit on the ground (or chair) and let yourself breathe very deeply. Feel the support of the earth under your feet. Feel your weight of gravity pulling you down to the floor. Feel your legs heavy and tired. Feel your body being calm. Notice what this feels like. (Continue for a couple minutes). Now you can wiggle around like normal. What do you notice?"

ART DIRECTIVES:
A. Bi-Lateral Scribble:
   Two handed Marker drawing (1 Marker/crayon for each hand): Each movement is done for 9-10 seconds. We encourage the children to look at their marks on the paper, the teacher can stand at the front of the group and demonstrate on the chalkboard, describing the process of bilateral scribbling **(Younger children may need help with taping and movements at first):**
   1. Tape Paper onto table (horizontally).
   2. Make Random Marks with both hands.
   3. Make Vertical Lines beginning from the bottom of the paper to the top, up and down. (can alternate hands).
   4. Make Horizontal Lines, across paper with each hand on opposite edge of page," bringing their markers to meet in the middle. Have children cross the midline (cross arms to opposite sides of the paper and back to opposite side of page-repeat)
   5. Make two Arcs, or windshield wiper movements, back and forth. Let the Arcs move into two large circles and go around and around.
   6. Continue to make Circles in the reverse direction,- reverse again/ repeating.

10 Start Up! Facilitator Manual

USING BOTH SIDES OF THE BODY / PARTNER DRAWING, HAND TRACING

WEEK 3

A. Bi-Lateral Scribble Cont.:
7. Make gentle Dots- now go up and down on the paper, now back and forth across the paper.
8. Put one arm and hand over the other and make a Big X and now move the other arm and hand on top, now the other on top (repeat 4-5 times)
9. Make Fast Circles, go around really fast, now gradually slower and smaller, until you have a small circle add dot in the middle of the smallest circle, and STOP.

B. Bi-Lateral Drawing:
Flip paper and re-tape paper to table
With markers in each hand children are instructed to:
1. Draw a groundline
2. Draw a dinosaur (or animal special to traditions of particular population, buffalo, whale, jaguar, etc. Include cultural teachings of animal)
3. Draw tree
4. Draw a sun
5. Draw another animal

MOTIVATION: "Who has hands?" We use our hands for many things? Think about all the good things you use your hands for and why that is important, which makes you important."

C. Partner Drawing
1. Have the child trace his partner's hands, then switch and traces the other's hands.
2. Children color in their own hands with markers, oil and chalk pastel.
3. Have children focus on what good things their hands do, and how this makes them feel important.
4. Think about their partner's hands and the good things they do with them.
5. Cut out hands from paper
6. Glue all hands on butcher paper to symbolize the class as a community
7. Can make an individual or group poem to go with image of hands.

CLOSURE/ DISCUSSION:

- Notice all of our hands together…all different sizes, shapes, colors. We are all unique. We are all special.

- It is important to honor that we are all different from each other and love each other because of our differences.

- Can each person say something positive about their partner and why their partner is special?" (This builds a child's esteem after a potentially traumatic weekend)

Facilitator Manual   Start Up!   11

WEEK 3

BODY TRACING

SELF PHASE

Purpose:
Physical Homeostasis

Goal:
Identity Formation/
Sensory Motor
Development

Neural Activity:
Cerebellum

Benefits:
• Building Self
  Concept
• Visual/spatial
  perception
• Community
  Building
• Building Esteem

Duration:
12 Weeks

Session 2 - Friday

ACTIVITY: BODY TRACING

Art Materials:
• Markers
• Largest paper for the desk space
• 2 Pieces each of 9x12 paper
• Large craft paper
• Acrylic Paint in cups
• Various Sized Brushes
• Water Cups
• Paper Towels

MUSIC FREEZE

BREATHING / MEDITATION
"Close your eyes or leave them open if you really need to. Breathe in deeply through your nose or mouth, until your lungs are full. Let your breath out until your lungs are empty. Sit comfortably, feel feet on the ground. Breathe in and imagine a white light filling your body. Let it out. Imagine a color that represents your stress. Where in your body is this stress color? Breathe in the white light and let it take over your stress. Breathe out the stress color. Breathe in white light into your entire body, from your toes to the top of your head." Can set a timer for longer and longer times, up to 3-5 minutes.

ART DIRECTIVES:
A. Bi-Lateral Scribble:
   Two handed Marker drawing (1 Marker/crayon for each hand):
Each movement is done for 9-10 seconds. We encourage the children to look at their marks on the paper, the teacher can stand at the front of the group and demonstrate on the chalkboard, describing the process of bilateral scribbling **(Younger children may need help with taping and movements at first):**
  1. Tape Paper onto table (horizontally).
  2. Make Random Marks with both hands.
  3. Make Vertical Lines beginning from the bottom of the paper to the top, up and down. (can alternate hands).
  4. Make Horizontal Lines, across paper with each hand on opposite edge of page," bringing their markers to meet in the middle. Have children cross the midline (cross arms to opposite sides of the paper and back to opposite side of page-repeat)

12 · Start Up! · Facilitator Manual

BODY TRACING

WEEK 3

A. Bi-Lateral Scribble Cont.:
5. Make two Arcs, or windshield wiper movements, back and forth. Let the Arcs move into two large circles and go around and around.
6. Continue to make Circles in the reverse direction,- reverse again/repeating.
7. Make gentle Dots- now go up and down on the paper, now back and forth across the paper.
8. Put one arm and hand over the other and make a Big X and now move the other arm and hand on top, now the other on top (repeat 4-5 times)
9. Make Fast Circles, go around really fast, now gradually slower and smaller, until you have a small circle add dot in the middle of the smallest circle, and STOP.

B. Bi-Lateral Drawing:
Flip paper and re-tape paper to table
With markers in each hand children are instructed to:
1. Draw a groundline
2. Draw a desert
3. Draw a cactus
4. Draw a tumbleweed
5. Draw a lizard
6. Draw a big rock
7. Draw a vulture in the sky

MOTIVATION: "Who knows of a person or a hero they admire? Why do you admire them? Today we are going to make ourselves into that person."

C. Partner Drawing
1. Body tracing- hang large craft paper on wall and have children outline each other's bodies.
2. Children can fill in clothes, hair, etc., with markers, pastel, and transform himself into a traditional tribal leader or cultural hero, positive political figure, superhero, rockstar, athlete, etc.
3. Children share body tracings with class.

CLOSURE/DISCUSSION:

- Who did you choose to draw yourself as and why?

- Did you like tracing the other person or being traced better? Why?

- What did you learn about yourself today?

Facilitator Manual   Start Up!

WEEK 4

PARTNER DRAWING

SELF PHASE

Purpose:
Physical Homeostasis

Goal:
Identity Formation/
Sensory Motor
Development

Neural Activity:
Cerebellum

Benefits:
- Perceptual Development
- Community Building
- Celebrating Diversity/ Uniqueness
- Visual/spatial perception
- Development of Social skills

Duration:
12 Weeks

Session 1 - Monday

ACTIVITY: PARTNER DRAWING (to enforce a sense of community)

Art Materials:
- Markers
- Largest paper for the desk space
- 3 Pieces each of 9x12 paper

SIMON SAYS

BREATHING / MEDITATION
"Breathe deeply, in and out slowly. Imagine you are a famous doctor or medicine person or curandera, and you save the lives of sick children. Everyone wants to come to you to have you help their children. Imagine how you would help these children and how it feels to do so."

ART DIRECTIVES:
A. Bi-Lateral Scribble:
Two handed Marker drawing (1 Marker/crayon for each hand): Each movement is done for 9-10 seconds. We encourage the children to look at their marks on the paper, the teacher can stand at the front of the group and demonstrate on the chalkboard, describing the process of bilateral scribbling **(Younger children may need help with taping and movements at first):**
1. Tape Paper onto table (horizontally).
2. Make Random Marks with both hands.
3. Make Vertical Lines beginning from the bottom of the paper to the top, up and down. (can alternate hands).
4. Make Horizontal Lines, across paper with each hand on opposite edge of page," bringing their markers to meet in the middle. Have children cross the midline (cross arms to opposite sides of the paper and back to opposite side of page-repeat)
5. Make two Arcs, or windshield wiper movements, back and forth. Let the Arcs move into two large circles and go around and around.
6. Continue to make Circles in the reverse direction,- reverse again/ repeating.
7. Make gentle Dots- now go up and down on the paper, now back and forth across the paper.
8. Put one arm and hand over the other and make a Big X and now move the other arm and hand on top, now the other on top (repeat 4-5 times)
9. Make Fast Circles, go around really fast, now gradually slower and smaller, until you have a small circle add dot in the middle of the smallest circle, and STOP.

Start Up! Facilitator Manual

PARTNER DRAWING

WEEK 4

B. Bi-Lateral Drawing:
Flip paper and re-tape paper to table
With markers in each hand children are instructed to:
1. Draw a groundline
2. Draw favorite animal
3. Draw tree
4. Draw a sun
5. Draw another animal of same type

MOTIVATION: "People are like snowflakes- no two are exactly alike, even twins have some differences. We are going to find unique and special things about our partners today when we draw each other, and honor our friends for this."

C. Partner Drawing
1. (New Paper) children pair up.
2. Draw picture of self
3. Draw Portrait of partner (one person pose, without looking at the paper.)
4. Switch and repeat.
5. Draw Portrait of partner looking at paper. (Switch and repeat)
6. Draw quick sketches of partner making different faces (mad, sad, happy, etc.)
7. Draw funny faces and different poses. (5-10 seconds each pose, can look at paper) (Switch and repeat)

CLOSURE/DISCUSSION:

- Did you like drawing another person?

- Did you like to be drawn?

- Which drawing did you like to make best? Why?

- What did you notice?

- Say something positive about your partner...

Facilitator Manual — Start Up! — 15

WEEK 4

STAMPING

SELF PHASE

Purpose:
Physical Homeostasis

Goal:
Identity Formation/
Sensory Motor
Development

Neural Activity:
Cerebellum

Benefits:
- Perceptual Development
- Community Building
- Celebrating Uniqueness/Diversity
- Cultivating Cultural Pride/Identity
- Eye-hand Coordination

Duration:
12 Weeks

Session 2 - Friday

ACTIVITY: STAMPING

Art Materials:
- Markers, (2 for each child)
- Largest paper for the desk space
- 2 Pieces each of 9x12 paper
- Bowls of Paint
- Small sponge pieces in paint bowls
- Large craft paper (rolled out on the floor or large table)

HEAD SHOULDERS KNEES & TOES

BREATHING / MEDITATION
"Breathe deeply, in and out slowly. Imagine you are a construction worker and you build beautiful houses and everyone wants you to build them a home. What kind of homes would you build? Tipis? Huts? Mud houses? What would you build it from? How would you decorate it? Imagine how it feels when you are done and a family moves in and thanks you for building their home."

ART DIRECTIVES:
A. Bi-Lateral Scribble:
   Two handed Marker drawing (1 Marker/crayon for each hand): Each movement is done for 9-10 seconds. We encourage the children to look at their marks on the paper, the teacher can stand at the front of the group and demonstrate on the chalkboard, describing the process of bilateral scribbling **(Younger children may need help with taping and movements at first):**
1. Tape Paper onto table (horizontally).
2. Make Random Marks with both hands.
3. Make Vertical Lines beginning from the bottom of the paper to the top, up and down. (can alternate hands).
4. Make Horizontal Lines, across paper with each hand on opposite edge of page," bringing their markers to meet in the middle. Have children cross the midline (cross arms to opposite sides of the paper and back to opposite side of page-repeat)
5. Make two Arcs, or windshield wiper movements, back and forth. Let the Arcs move into two large circles and go around and around.
6. Continue to make Circles in the reverse direction,- reverse again/repeating.

Start Up! Facilitator Manual

STAMPING

WEEK 4

A. Bi-Lateral Scribble Cont.:
7. Make gentle Dots- now go up and down on the paper, now back and forth across the paper.
8. Put one arm and hand over the other and make a Big X and now move the other arm and hand on top, now the other on top (repeat 4-5 times)
9. Make Fast Circles, go around really fast, now gradually slower and smaller, until you have a small circle add dot in the middle of the smallest circle, and STOP.

B. Bi-Lateral Drawing:
Flip paper and re-tape paper to table
With markers in each hand children are instructed to:
1. Draw a sky
2. Draw a moon
3. Draw stars
4. Draw planets
5. Draw a spaceship
6. Draw a star being (alien)

MOTIVATION: Fun, build community, engage sense of touch (tactile). Does anyone know what our Tribal flag looks like? Does anyone know what this traditional symbol means? "It's important to feel proud of who we are as a people….this flag symbolizes our Tribe…be proud of it."

C. Stamping a Traditional Symbol or Tribal Flag
(Medicine wheel, etc)
1. Have an outline of a traditional Tribal/Cultural Symbol or Flag pre-drawn on large craft paper and rolled out onto he floor or long table. If large class, have 2 symbols on 2 different pieces of craft paper and split into 2 groups.
2. Have a few children on each color paint begin to fill in the symbols with paint sponges.
3. ***Teacher:* Can include the stories and cultural teachings about the symbols and flags.**

CLOSURE/ DISCUSSION:

- Did you like the way the paint sponges felt in your hands?

- Did you like working within a group?

- What did you learn about the traditional symbol or flag from your culture?

- What did you learn about yourself today?

Facilitator Manual — Start Up!

WEEK 5

RELEASING FEELINGS MEDITATION/ CHALK PASTEL DRAWING

SELF PHASE

Purpose:
Physical Homeostasis

Goal:
Identity Formation/ Sensory Motor Development

Neural Activity:
Cerebellum

Benefits:
- Development of Imagination
- Normalize emotions
- Emotional Recognition
- Emotional Containment
- Learning adaptive coping strategies
- Emotional Release
- Development of Abstract Thinking

Duration:
12 Weeks

Session 1 - Monday

ACTIVITY: RELEASING FEELINGS MEDITATION/ CHALK PASTEL DRAWING

Art Materials:
- Markers
- Largest paper for the desk space
- 2 Pieces each of 9x12 paper
- Chalk Pastels

HEAD SHOULDERS KNEES &TOES

BREATHING / MEDITATION
"Breathe deeply, in and out slowly. Think about something that makes you happy. Feel the happiness and breathe it into your entire body."

ART DIRECTIVES:
A. Bi-Lateral Scribble:
   Two handed Marker drawing (1 Marker/crayon for each hand): Each movement is done for 9-10 seconds. We encourage the children to look at their marks on the paper, the teacher can stand at the front of the group and demonstrate on the chalkboard, describing the process of bilateral scribbling **(Younger children may need help with taping and movements at first):**
  1. Tape Paper onto table (horizontally).
  2. Make Random Marks with both hands.
  3. Make Vertical Lines beginning from the bottom of the paper to the top, up and down. (can alternate hands).
  4. Make Horizontal Lines, across paper with each hand on opposite edge of page," bringing their markers to meet in the middle. Have children cross the midline (cross arms to opposite sides of the paper and back to opposite side of page-repeat)
  5. Make two Arcs, or windshield wiper movements, back and forth. Let the Arcs move into two large circles and go around and around.
  6. Continue to make Circles in the reverse direction,- reverse again/ repeating.
  7. Make gentle Dots- now go up and down on the paper, now back and forth across the paper.
  8. Put one arm and hand over the other and make a Big X and now move the other arm and hand on top, now the other on top (repeat 4-5 times)
  9. Make Fast Circles, go around really fast, now gradually slower and smaller, until you have a small circle add dot in the middle of the smallest circle, and STOP.

Start Up!   Facilitator Manual

RELEASING FEELINGS MEDITATION/ CHALK PASTEL DRAWING

WEEK 5

B. Bi-Lateral Drawing:
Flip paper and re-tape paper to table
With markers in each hand children are instructed to:
1. Draw a ground line
2. Draw a jungle of trees
3. Draw a monkey
4. Draw a tiger
5. Draw a river
6. Draw a parrot
7. Draw fish in the river

MOTIVATION: "Raise your hand if you ever have feelings inside you that you wish you could get rid of? Today we are going to release those feelings onto paper."

C. Releasing Feelings Meditation/ Chalk Pastel Drawing
1. Have children close their eyes
2. Breathe deeply through nose
3. "Relax toes, feet, calves, thighs, stomach, chest, shoulders, arms, neck, face"
4. "Feel your body feeling heavy in your seat, like a bag of cement"
5. "Are there any places which feel tight or uncomfortable?
6. Imagine a golden light and breathe into those uncomfortable places.
7. Imagine those uncomfortable places or any unpleasant feelings as a color and blow this color out of your mouth and away from your body.
8. Imagine a soothing, healing color filling up your whole body starting with your toes, feet, calves, thighs, stomach, chest, shoulders, arms, neck, face. Breathe deeply and feel the healing power this light has."
9. Draw their healing color/colors with chalk pastel and blend it with their hands.

CLOSURE/ DISCUSSION:

• Was that hard or easy?

• What did you like least?

• What did you like most?

• You can do this at any time when you are needing to relax or heal yourself. You have the power to do this.

Facilitator Manual — Start Up! — 19

WEEK 5

A SAFE PLACE/A ROOM OF YOUR OWN

SELF PHASE

Purpose:
Physical Homeostasis

Goal:
Identity Formation/
Sensory Motor
Development

Neural Activity:
Cerebellum

Benefits:
- Eye-hand Coordination
- Transforming negative to positive
- Emotional Recognition
- Emotional Containment
- Creating Safety

Duration:
12 Weeks

Session 2 - Friday

ACTIVITY: A SAFE PLACE/A ROOM OF YOUR OWN

Art Materials:
- Markers
- Largest paper for the desk space
- Shoe boxes/small boxes
- Clay
- Magazines
- Wood (Small Scraps)
- Fabric Scraps etc

MUSIC FREEZE

BREATHING / MEDITATION
"Breathe deeply, in and out slowly. Imagine you are sitting in a meadow. The sun is shining and there is a light, warm rain coming down. You look up see a rainbow shining brightly right over your head. It is beautiful and radiant, shining its rainbow light down into your body, making you feel calm and peaceful."

ART DIRECTIVES:
A. Bi-Lateral Scribble:
   Two handed Marker drawing (1 Marker/crayon for each hand):
Each movement is done for 9-10 seconds. We encourage the children to look at their marks on the paper, the teacher can stand at the front of the group and demonstrate on the chalkboard, describing the process of bilateral scribbling **(Younger children may need help with taping and movements at first):**
  1. Tape Paper onto table (horizontally).
  2. Make Random Marks with both hands.
  3. Make Vertical Lines beginning from the bottom of the paper to the top, up and down. (can alternate hands).
  4. Make Horizontal Lines, across paper with each hand on opposite edge of page," bringing their markers to meet in the middle. Have children cross the midline (cross arms to opposite sides of the paper and back to opposite side of page-repeat)
  5. Make two Arcs, or windshield wiper movements, back and forth. Let the Arcs move into two large circles and go around and around.

Start Up!   Facilitator Manual

A SAFE PLACE/A ROOM OF YOUR OWN

WEEK 5

A. Bi-Lateral Scribble Cont.:
6. Continue to make Circles in the reverse direction,- reverse again/ repeating.
7. Make gentle Dots- now go up and down on the paper, now back and forth across the paper.
8. Put one arm and hand over the other and make a Big X and now move the other arm and hand on top, now the other on top (repeat 4-5 times)
9. Make Fast Circles, go around really fast, now gradually slower and smaller, until you have a small circle add dot in the middle of the smallest circle, and STOP.

B. Bi-Lateral Drawing:
Flip paper and re-tape paper to table
With markers in each hand children are instructed to:
1. Draw Waterline
2. Draw Mountains
3. Draw birds
4. Draw fish in the river

MOTIVATION: "Having a place where you can feel safe is very important. Today you are going to design your own room and make it exactly the way you want it."

C. Room of your Own
1. Decorate the inside of your box as your ideal room
2. How big would your room be? What kind of furniture would you have?
3. Make furniture with found objects, clay, wood, spools, buttons
4. Draw pictures to decorate, magazine pictures
5. ***Teacher:*** **"This is a safe place for you and only you to be. It is your safe place and no one can come in unless you give permission."**
6. Share art work with classmates.

CLOSURE/ DISCUSSION:

- What was hard/what was easy?

- What was your favorite part?

- How did it feel to have a safe place all your own?

WEEK 6

CONNECT WITH NATURE

SELF PHASE

Purpose:
Physical Homeostasis

Goal:
Identity Formation/
Sensory Motor
Development

Neural Activity:
Cerebellum

Benefits:
• Self expression
• Community Building
• Connecting with Nature
• Color and Composition

Duration:
12 Weeks

Session 1 - Monday

ACTIVITY: CONNECT WITH NATURE

Art Materials:
• Markers
• 3 Pieces each of 9 x 12 paper
• Construction paper
• Glue

SIMON SAYS

BREATHING / MEDITATION
"Breathe deeply, in and out slowly. Imagine you are sitting by a little stream. You can hear the water flowing by. Water is life. Nothing can live without water. Water can heal. Imagine the water giving you a message, saying something healing to you, just what you need to hear today. Thank the water for this message."

ART DIRECTIVES:
A. Bi-Lateral Scribble:
   Two handed Marker drawing (1 Marker/crayon for each hand): Each movement is done for 9-10 seconds. We encourage the children to look at their marks on the paper, the teacher can stand at the front of the group and demonstrate on the chalkboard, describing the process of bilateral scribbling **(Younger children may need help with taping and movements at first):**
  1. Tape Paper onto table (horizontally).
  2. Make Random Marks with both hands.
  3. Make Vertical Lines beginning from the bottom of the paper to the top, up and down. (can alternate hands).
  4. Make Horizontal Lines, across paper with each hand on opposite edge of page," bringing their markers to meet in the middle. Have children cross the midline (cross arms to opposite sides of the paper and back to opposite side of page-repeat)
  5. Make two Arcs, or windshield wiper movements, back and forth. Let the Arcs move into two large circles and go around and around.
  6. Continue to make Circles in the reverse direction,- reverse again/ repeating.
  7. Make gentle Dots- now go up and down on the paper, now back and forth across the paper.
  8. Put one arm and hand over the other and make a Big X and now move the other arm and hand on top, now the other on top (repeat 4-5 times)
  9. Make Fast Circles, go around really fast, now gradually slower and smaller, until you have a small circle add dot in the middle of the smallest circle, and STOP.

22   Start Up!   Facilitator Manual

CONNECT WITH NATURE

WEEK 6

B. Bi-Lateral Drawing:
Flip paper and re-tape paper to table
With markers in each hand children are instructed to:
1. Draw a groundline
2. Draw a house from another culture with windows and door (tipi, wigwam, hut, traditional home, can add cultural teachings about traditional homes of particular population)
3. Draw a tree
4. Draw a basket of apples underneath the tree (or can be traditional food and add cultural teachings about the traditional foods of particular population)
5. Put clouds up in the sky
6. Sun / Birds

MOTIVATION: "Who loves to be outside? Who feels connected to things in nature? Trees ? Water ? Animals ? Nature has a powerful calming force. Today we are going for a walk outside to feel that powerful force and to gather things from nature to make art with. Choose things that make you feel good."

C. Connect with Nature
1. Walk outside in nature
2. Hear the sounds around you.
3. See what is around you.
4. Feel your connection to Mother Earth (Ina Maka, Pacha Mama or traditional name used for Mother Earth)
5. Deep breathe
6. *Teacher:* **Include traditional cultural teachings and stories about Mother Earth from your people. Ask children to offer tobacco or say "thank you" to Mother Earth in exchange for what they take.**
7. Collect nature materials to glue to construction paper

CLOSURE/ DISCUSSION:

- What did you see?

- What did you hear?

- What item that your collected from nature was your favorite?

- What did you notice or learn about yourself today?

WEEK 6

A SAFE PLACE MEDITATION/ART WITH ANCESTORS

SELF PHASE

Purpose:
Physical Homeostasis

Goal:
Identity Formation/
Sensory Motor
Development

Neural Activity:
Cerebellum

Benefits:
- Promotes Relaxation
- Celebrating Uniqueness/Diversity
- Cultivating Cultural Pride/Identity
- Creating Safety
- Learning adaptive coping strategies
- Empowerment/ Esteem Building
- Relaxation
- Development of Abstract Thinking
- Development of Imagination

Duration:
12 Weeks

Session 2 - Friday

ACTIVITY: A SAFE PLACE MEDITATION/ART WITH ANCESTORS

Art Materials:
- Markers
- Oil Pastels
- Chalk Pastels
- Largest paper for the desk space
- 3 Pieces each of 9 x 12 paper

HEAD SHOULDERS KNEES &TOES

BREATHING / MEDITATION
"Breathe deeply, in and out slowly. Imagine laying on a beach, feeling the warm sand beneath you. Your body feels heavy as it presses into the earth. You look up and see the sun. Nothing can live without the sun; it gives our bodies energy, it helps plants to grow, and keeps our earth warm. Look up into the sun and feels its warmth radiating into your body. Feel it giving you energy. Thank the sun for your life."

ART DIRECTIVES:
A. Bi-Lateral Scribble:

Two handed Marker drawing (1 Marker/crayon for each hand): Each movement is done for 9-10 seconds. We encourage the children to look at their marks on the paper, the teacher can stand at the front of the group and demonstrate on the chalkboard, describing the process of bilateral scribbling **(Younger children may need help with taping and movements at first):**

1. Tape Paper onto table (horizontally).
2. "When I say GO- make Random Marks with both hands, until I say STOP."
3. "When I say GO- make Vertical Lines beginning from the bottom of the paper to the top, up and down- repeating until I say STOP" (can alternate hands).
4. "When I say GO- make Horizontal Lines, across paper with each hand on opposite edge of page," bringing their markers to meet in the middle. Have children cross the midline (cross arms to opposite sides of the paper and back to opposite side of page-repeat) "Until I say STOP."
5. "When I say GO- make two Arcs, or windshield wiper movements, back and forth. Let the Arcs move into two large circles and go around and around, until I say STOP."

Start Up!   Facilitator Manual

A SAFE PLACE MEDITATION/ART WITH ANCESTORS

WEEK 6

A. Bi-Lateral Scribble Cont.:
6. Continue to make Circles in the reverse direction,- reverse again/ repeating.
7. Make gentle Dots- now go up and down on the paper, now back and forth across the paper.
8. Put one arm and hand over the other and make a Big X and now move the other arm and hand on top, now the other on top (repeat 4-5 times)
9. Make Fast Circles, go around really fast, now gradually slower and smaller, until you have a small circle add dot in the middle of the smallest circle, and STOP.

B. Bi-Lateral Drawing:
Flip paper and re-tape paper to table
With markers in each hand children are instructed to:
1. Draw a starry
2. Draw some star people (can add cultural teachings about traditional star knowledge beliefs of particular population)
3. Draw a spaceship
4. Draw a moon

MOTIVATION: "What is an ancestor? Do you remember your ancestors through pictures or stories your family tells? Today we are going to use our imaginations to remember our ancestors."

C. A Safe Place Meditation/Art with Ancestors
1. Progressive relaxation- (close eyes) relax your toes, ankles, knees, lower torso, upper torso, neck, arms, face, head.
2. Think of your favorite ancestor (can be someone from your family or from your people.)
3. Feel that ancestor protecting you. This ancestor might have a message for you, listen.
4. Feel what that protection feels like. Do this for as long as you can before class becomes restless.
5. Draw the ancestor on paper.
6. Have children share their images, if they choose.

CLOSURE/DISCUSSION:

- How did this feel?

- What did you notice or learn about yourself today?

- You can do this wherever you are: you can bring back this sense of protection and safety at any time… when you are feeling afraid, lonely, sad, etc or when you need extra strength, like if you want to win a race.

Facilitator Manual — Start Up!

WEEK 7

POWER ANIMAL NECKLACES

SELF PHASE

Purpose:
Physical Homeostasis

Goal:
Identity Formation/
Sensory Motor
Development

Neural Activity:
Cerebellum

Benefits:
• Promotes Relaxation
• Celebrating
  Uniqueness/Diversity
• Creating Safety
• Learning Adaptive
  Coping Strategies
• Empowerment/
  Esteem Building
• Development of
  Abstract Thinking
• Development of
  Imagination

Duration:
12 Weeks

Session 1 - Monday

ACTIVITY: POWER ANIMAL NECKLACES

Art Materials:
• Markers
• Drum
• Model Magic Clay (1/2 pkg per child)
• 1 Piece each of 9 x 12 paper

MUSIC FREEZE

BREATHING / MEDITATION
"Breathe deeply, in and out slowly. Imagine you are sitting around a campfire. You feel the heat emanating from the fire and you see the glow against the night sky. You feel warm and at peace. Think of the various ways people use fire to live; for heat, for cooking, etc. Fire is strong- it can burn down a forest. But forests need to burn down once in awhile to be healthy. Like forests, people also have difficult things happen, which make us stronger. Listen to the crackle of the fire, there is a voice within that fire that is giving you a message of strength. It is a message you need to hear today."

ART DIRECTIVES:
A. Bi-Lateral Scribble:
   Two handed Marker drawing (1 Marker/crayon for each hand): Each movement is done for 9-10 seconds. We encourage the children to look at their marks on the paper, the teacher can stand at the front of the group and demonstrate on the chalkboard, describing the process of bilateral scribbling **(Younger children may need help with taping and movements at first):**
  1. Tape Paper onto table (horizontally).
  2. Make Random Marks with both hands.
  3. Make Vertical Lines beginning from the bottom of the paper to the top, up and down. (can alternate hands).
  4. Make Horizontal Lines, across paper with each hand on opposite edge of page," bringing their markers to meet in the middle. Have children cross the midline (cross arms to opposite sides of the paper and back to opposite side of page-repeat)
  5. Make two Arcs, or windshield wiper movements, back and forth. Let the Arcs move into two large circles and go around and around.
  6. Continue to make Circles in the reverse direction,- reverse again/ repeating.
  7. Make gentle Dots- now go up and down on the paper, now back and forth across the paper.
  8. Put one arm and hand over the other and make a Big X and now move the other arm and hand on top, now the other on top (repeat 4-5 times)

Start Up! Facilitator Manual

POWER ANIMAL NECKLACES

WEEK 7

A. Bi-Lateral Scribble Cont.:
9. Make Fast Circles, go around really fast, now gradually slower and smaller, until you have a small circle add dot in the middle of the smallest circle, and STOP.

B. Bi-Lateral Drawing:
Flip paper and re-tape paper to table
With markers in each hand children are instructed to:
1. Draw a waterline
2. Draw a boat (can be a traditional boat of particular population and add cultural teachings)
3. Draw a motor or sails to the boat (if applicable)
4. Draw a flag
5. Draw someone fishing with a line in the water with a hook
6. Draw some fish in the water
7. Add a shark
8. Draw a starfish in the water
9. Add clouds/sun/birds

MOTIVATION: Do you have a favorite animal? Sometimes we like a particular animal because it gives us strength or protection. We call these "power animals." Today you are going on a journey to meet your power animal.

C. Power Animals Necklaces
1. Drum for the children as they sit in their seats with their heads down.
2. While drumming. lead the children on a meditation….
3. "Imagine you are on the top of a mountain by yourself. You are feeling very relaxed. You are looking up at the sky and you see the clouds, you see trees, you feel the grass beneath you. You feel the gentle breeze blowing your hair.
4. "Now imagine you see an animal far off in the distance. You see this animal coming toward you and you know this animal is nice, and is coming to visit with you. This animal stands in front of you and begins to speak to you. It tells you something and shows you something. (Let several minutes go by only drumming) "After your animal has finished giving you its message, say thank you to it and say good bye as the animal leaves."
5. Slowly stop the drumming.
6. Ask the children to sculpt the animal that visited them with clay. (You can turn on soft music while they sculpt).
7. Make sure the children make a hole with a tip of a pencil, big enough for yarn to easily fit through to connect their sculptures to a necklace when dried and painted.
8. *Teacher:* **Make sure to make extras of various animals for any student who might be absent so the student will have something to paint next session.**

CLOSURE/ DISCUSSION:

- What animal came to you?

- What emotions came up when visiting this animal?

- What did you notice or learn about yourself today?

Facilitator Manual — Start Up!

WEEK 7

PAINTING POWER ANIMALS/ATTACHING TO A NECKLACE

SELF PHASE

Purpose:
Physical Homeostasis

Goal:
Identity Formation/ Sensory Motor Development

Neural Activity:
Cerebellum

Benefits:
- Delaying gratification
- Patience
- Learning adaptive coping strategies
- Empowerment/ Esteem Building
- Eye-hand Coordination

Duration:
12 Weeks

Session 2 - Friday

ACTIVITY: PAINTING POWER ANIMALS/ATTACHING TO A NECKLACE

Art Materials:
- Markers
- Paint in cups
- Brushes
- Yarn
- 1 Piece each of 9 x 12 paper

SIMON SAYS

BREATHING / MEDITATION
"Imagine you are on the top of a mountain by yourself. You are feeling very relaxed. You are looking up at the sky and you see the clouds, you see trees, you feel the grass beneath you. You feel the gentle breeze blowing your hair. Now imagine you see your power animal coming toward you. You know this animal; it is familiar, an old friend, and it is coming to visit with you. Your power animal stands in front of you and begins to speak to you. It tells you something good about yourself. (Let a couple minutes go by in silence) "After your animal has finished giving you its message, say thank you to it and say good bye as the animal leaves."

ART DIRECTIVES:
A. Bi-Lateral Scribble:
   Two handed Marker drawing (1 Marker/crayon for each hand): Each movement is done for 9-10 seconds. We encourage the children to look at their marks on the paper, the teacher can stand at the front of the group and demonstrate on the chalkboard, describing the process of bilateral scribbling **(Younger children may need help with taping and movements at first):**
  1. Tape Paper onto table (horizontally).
  2. Make Random Marks with both hands.
  3. Make Vertical Lines beginning from the bottom of the paper to the top, up and down. (can alternate hands).
  4. Make Horizontal Lines, across paper with each hand on opposite edge of page," bringing their markers to meet in the middle. Have children cross the midline (cross arms to opposite sides of the paper and back to opposite side of page-repeat)
  5. Make two Arcs, or windshield wiper movements, back and forth. Let the Arcs move into two large circles and go around and around.
  6. Continue to make Circles in the reverse direction,- reverse again/ repeating.
  7. Make gentle Dots- now go up and down on the paper, now back and forth across the paper.

Start Up!   Facilitator Manual

PAINTING POWER ANIMALS/ATTACHING TO A NECKLACE — WEEK 7

A. Bi-Lateral Scribble Cont.:
8. Put one arm and hand over the other and make a Big X and now move the other arm and hand on top, now the other on top (repeat 4-5 times)
9. Make Fast Circles, go around really fast, now gradually slower and smaller, until you have a small circle add dot in the middle of the smallest circle, and STOP.

B. Bi-Lateral Drawing:
Flip paper and re-tape paper to table
With markers in each hand children are instructed to:
1. Draw a groundline
2. Draw a dinosaur (or animal special to traditions of particular population, buffalo, whale, jaguar, etc. Include cultural teachings of animal)
3. Draw tree
4. Draw a sun
5. Draw another animal

MOTIVATION: "Remember your journey meeting your power animal last time. Today we are going to remember that journey and the feeling we had from our power animals. Those animals gave us medicine to help us and heal us. By making a necklace of your animal, you are honoring this animal by wearing this medicine around your neck. It will help you be strong. Even if you lose this necklace, this medicine will always be with you."

C. Painting Power Animals/Attaching to a Necklace
1. Have the children paint their power animal sculptures they made last week.
2. Let the paint dry then attach yarn through the hole in sculpture.
3. Let the children wear their power animal necklaces.
4. **Teacher: Emphasize how each child has received different strength and medicine from their power animal and how special that is. Remind them they will have this medicine for the rest of their lives and can feel it whenever they feel upset etc. Even if they lose their necklaces, assure them their animal is still there to protect them.**
5. Have children share their necklaces if they wish.

CLOSURE/ DISCUSSION:

- What did you like best about this experience?
- What did you like least?
- What did you notice or learn about yourself today?

Facilitator Manual — Start Up!

WEEK 8

ECO ART

SELF PHASE

Purpose:
Physical Homeostasis

Goal:
Identity Formation/
Sensory Motor
Development

Neural Activity:
Cerebellum

Benefits:
- Eye-hand coordination
- Perceptual Development
- Transforming negative to positive
- Visual/spatial perception

Duration:
12 Weeks

Session 1 - Monday

ACTIVITY: ECO ART

Art Materials:
- Markers
- Masking Tape
- Paint in cups
- Brushes
- 1 Piece each of 9 x 12 paper
- Toothpaste/Tea boxes
- Coffee cans, and any saved materials

HEAD SHOULDERS KNEES & TOES

BREATHING / MEDITATION
"Take deep breaths into your lungs and out of your lungs. Imagine the world around you. Look and see what is happening to your culture and your people, the animals, and the land around you. Imagine that you are a very famous inventor and you are going to build an invention to help your people, the animals, and/or the land. What invention will you make? Take a few breaths to think about this."

ART DIRECTIVES:
A. Bi-Lateral Scribble:
   Two handed Marker drawing (1 Marker/crayon for each hand): Each movement is done for 9-10 seconds. We encourage the children to look at their marks on the paper, the teacher can stand at the front of the group and demonstrate on the chalkboard, describing the process of bilateral scribbling **(Younger children may need help with taping and movements at first):**
   1. Tape Paper onto table (horizontally).
   2. Make Random Marks with both hands.
   3. Make Vertical Lines beginning from the bottom of the paper to the top, up and down. (can alternate hands).
   4. Make Horizontal Lines, across paper with each hand on opposite edge of page," bringing their markers to meet in the middle. Have children cross the midline (cross arms to opposite sides of the paper and back to opposite side of page-repeat)
   5. Make two Arcs, or windshield wiper movements, back and forth. Let the Arcs move into two large circles and go around and around.

ECO ART

WEEK 8

A. Bi-Lateral Scribble Cont.:
6. Continue to make Circles in the reverse direction,- reverse again/ repeating.
7. Make gentle Dots- now go up and down on the paper, now back and forth across the paper.
8. Put one arm and hand over the other and make a Big X and now move the other arm and hand on top, now the other on top (repeat 4-5 times)
9. Make Fast Circles, go around really fast, now gradually slower and smaller, until you have a small circle add dot in the middle of the smallest circle, and STOP.

B. Bi-Lateral Drawing:
Flip paper and re-tape paper to table
With markers in each hand children are instructed to:
1. Draw a groundline
2. Draw some flowers
3. Draw some ladybugs
4. Draw some spiders
5. Draw some mosquitoes

MOTIVATION: "Have you ever wanted to make an invention? Today we are each going to make an invention from our imaginations that will somehow help the world. We will make these from recycled materials found from our own homes."

C. Eco Art
1. Have children tape boxes and recycled materials together to create an invention of their choice.
2. When sculpture is complete have the children paint them.
3. Share inventions with class.

CLOSURE/ DISCUSSION:

- What was most enjoyable?

- Least enjoyable?

- What did you notice or learn about yourself today?

Facilitator Manual — Start Up!

WEEK 8

MAKE A MAGIC HAT

SELF PHASE

Purpose:
Physical Homeostasis

Goal:
Identity Formation/
Sensory Motor
Development

Neural Activity:
Cerebellum

Benefits:
- Eye-hand coordination
- Developing altruism
- Community Building
- Perceptual Development
- Development of Imagination

Duration:
12 Weeks

Session 2 - Friday

ACTIVITY: MAKE A MAGIC HAT

Art Materials:
- Markers
- Masking Tape
- Glue
- Scissors
- Construction paper
- Recycled materials- fabric, buttons, etc
- Glitter, etc
- 1Piece each of 9 x 12 paper

MUSIC FREEZE

BREATHING / MEDITATION
"Sit very still and breathe deeply. Feel yourself very relaxed. Imagine your heart in your chest growing with a feeling of love for yourself. Imagine your heart glowing bright green and the green light of love shining out from your chest area. Now imagine loving the whole world and bringing that green light from your heart out into space and imagine it covering the entire earth and everything on earth, plants, animals and people can feel your love. Breathe deeply and feel the strength of your love healing the planet."

ART DIRECTIVES:
A. Bi-Lateral Scribble:
   Two handed Marker drawing (1 Marker/crayon for each hand): Each movement is done for 9-10 seconds. We encourage the children to look at their marks on the paper, the teacher can stand at the front of the group and demonstrate on the chalkboard, describing the process of bilateral scribbling **(Younger children may need help with taping and movements at first):**
   1. Tape Paper onto table (horizontally).
   2. Make Random Marks with both hands.
   3. Make Vertical Lines beginning from the bottom of the paper to the top, up and down. (can alternate hands).
   4. Make Horizontal Lines, across paper with each hand on opposite edge of page," bringing their markers to meet in the middle. Have children cross the midline (cross arms to opposite sides of the paper and back to opposite side of page-repeat)
   5. Make two Arcs, or windshield wiper movements, back and forth. Let the Arcs move into two large circles and go around and around.
   6. Continue to make Circles in the reverse direction,- reverse again/ repeating.

Start Up!   Facilitator Manual

MAKE A MAGIC HAT

WEEK 8

A. Bi-Lateral Scribble Cont.:
7. Make gentle Dots- now go up and down on the paper, now back and forth across the paper.
8. Put one arm and hand over the other and make a Big X and now move the other arm and hand on top, now the other on top (repeat 4-5 times)
9. Make Fast Circles, go around really fast, now gradually slower and smaller, until you have a small circle add dot in the middle of the smallest circle, and STOP.

B. Bi-Lateral Drawing:
Flip paper and re-tape paper to table
With markers in each hand children are instructed to:
1. Draw a groundline
2. Draw a cactus
3. Draw a desert
4. Draw a skull
5. Draw another cactus
6. Draw a coyote
7. Draw a moon

MOTIVATION: "Why do people wear hats? How do you feel when wearing a hat? Today we are going to make a hat for a friend. You are going to put all your love and support in this hat your friend feels your love and support when wearing it."

C. Make a Magic Hat
1. Partner children in two's who do not know each other well
2. Tape different colored construction paper and recycled materials together to create a magic hat.
3. Children can exchange hats when both are complete.
4. ***Teacher:* "Put all your good feelings, thoughts, and prayers into these hats. Wish for good things for yourself and your friends, even some one you do not know very well."**
5. Share hats with class.

CLOSURE/ DISCUSSION:

- How did it feel to make a hat for your classmate?

- What did you like most? Least? Was this easy or hard?

- What did you notice or learn about yourself today?

Facilitator Manual   Start Up!

WEEK 9

PARTNER DRAWING

SELF PHASE

Purpose:
Physical Homeostasis

Goal:
Identity Formation/
Sensory Motor
Development

Neural Activity:
Cerebellum

Benefits:
- Community Building
- Cultural Identity
- Creating Trust
- Eye-hand coordination

Duration:
12 Weeks

Session 1 - Monday

ACTIVITY: PARTNER DRAWING
(repetition is necessary for re-building neural pathways)

Art Materials:
- Markers
- 3Piece each of 9 x 12 paper

SIMON SAYS

BREATHING / MEDITATION
Close your eyes and breathe deeply. Imagine all your classmates in the same room with you. You may know some of them well, and others, you may not know very well. Some you may like and others you may not like as much. Think about how each child in your class has something special, that you are all important and all have a special talent to contribute to the world. Feel that green light of love shining from your heart and imagine it shining into each of your classmates."

ART DIRECTIVES:
A. Bi-Lateral Scribble:
   Two handed Marker drawing (1 Marker/crayon for each hand): Each movement is done for 9-10 seconds. We encourage the children to look at their marks on the paper, the teacher can stand at the front of the group and demonstrate on the chalkboard, describing the process of bilateral scribbling **(Younger children may need help with taping and movements at first):**
   1. Tape Paper onto table (horizontally).
   2. Make Random Marks with both hands.
   3. Make Vertical Lines beginning from the bottom of the paper to the top, up and down. (can alternate hands).
   4. Make Horizontal Lines, across paper with each hand on opposite edge of page," bringing their markers to meet in the middle. Have children cross the midline (cross arms to opposite sides of the paper and back to opposite side of page-repeat)
   5. Make two Arcs, or windshield wiper movements, back and forth. Let the Arcs move into two large circles and go around and around.
   6. Continue to make Circles in the reverse direction,- reverse again/ repeating.

34   Start Up!   Facilitator Manual

PARTNER DRAWING

WEEK 9

A. Bi-Lateral Scribble:
7. Make gentle Dots- now go up and down on the paper, now back and forth across the paper.
8. Put one arm and hand over the other and make a Big X and now move the other arm and hand on top, now the other on top (repeat 4-5 times)
9. Make Fast Circles, go around really fast, now gradually slower and smaller, until you have a small circle add dot in the middle of the smallest circle, and STOP.

B. Bi-Lateral Drawing:
Flip paper and re-tape paper to table
With markers in each hand children are instructed to:
1. Draw Waterline
2. Draw Mountains
3. Draw birds
4. Draw fish in the river

MOTIVATION: "It is fun to draw and not be attached to what it looks like. Today we will draw our friends in partner drawing. Don't worry about how it looks, just have fun and get to know your partner a little more."

C. Partner Drawing
1. Choose a partner you have not worked with before.
2. Draw your partner (you can look at the paper)
3. Draw your partner again (not looking at the paper)
4. Try drawing with the other hand.
5. Draw your partner making funny poses.
6. Draw your partner making funny faces.
7. Switch and the other draws, and the other poses.
8. Share drawings with class. (This usually produces some laughs)

CLOSURE/ DISCUSSION:

- How did it feel to draw your classmate?
- What did you like most? Least?
- Was this easy or hard?
- What did you notice or learn about yourself today?

Facilitator Manual — Start Up!

WEEK 9

PACKING PEANUT SCULPTURE

SELF PHASE

Purpose:
Physical Homeostasis

Goal:
Identity Formation/
Sensory Motor
Development

Neural Activity:
Cerebellum

Benefits:
• Visual/spatial
   perception
• Eye-hand
   coordination
• Self expression
• Development of
   Imagination

Duration:
12 Weeks

Session 2 - Friday

ACTIVITY: PACKING PEANUT SCULPTURE

Art Materials:
• Markers
• Packing peanuts
• Toothpicks
• Paint
• 3 Pieces each of 9 x 12 paper

HEAD SHOULDERS KNEES & TOES

BREATHING / MEDITATION
"Breathe deeply into your lungs and out of your lungs. If there is any worry or stress, notice where it is in your body. Breathe deeply into these places and imagine all the worry or stress getting smaller and smaller with each breath. Imagine yourself very strong and able to handle any difficult situation that may arise."

ART DIRECTIVES:
A. Bi-Lateral Scribble:
   Two handed Marker drawing (1 Marker/crayon for each hand): Each movement is done for 9-10 seconds. We encourage the children to look at their marks on the paper, the teacher can stand at the front of the group and demonstrate on the chalkboard, describing the process of bilateral scribbling **(Younger children may need help with taping and movements at first):**
   1. Tape Paper onto table (horizontally).
   2. Make Random Marks with both hands.
   3. Make Vertical Lines beginning from the bottom of the paper to the top, up and down. (can alternate hands).
   4. Make Horizontal Lines, across paper with each hand on opposite edge of page," bringing their markers to meet in the middle. Have children cross the midline (cross arms to opposite sides of the paper and back to opposite side of page-repeat)
   5. Make two Arcs, or windshield wiper movements, back and forth. Let the Arcs move into two large circles and go around and around.

Start Up! Facilitator Manual

PACKING PEANUT SCULPTURE
WEEK 9

A. Bi-Lateral Scribble Cont.:
6. Continue to make Circles in the reverse direction,- reverse again/ repeating.
7. Make gentle Dots- now go up and down on the paper, now back and forth across the paper.
8. Put one arm and hand over the other and make a Big X and now move the other arm and hand on top, now the other on top (repeat 4-5 times)
9. Make Fast Circles, go around really fast, now gradually slower and smaller, until you have a small circle add dot in the middle of the smallest circle, and STOP.

B. Bi-Lateral Drawing:
Flip paper and re-tape paper to table
With markers in each hand children are instructed to:
1. Draw a sky
2. Draw a moon
3. Draw stars
4. Draw planets
5. Draw a spaceship
6. Draw a star being (alien)

MOTIVATION: "Have you ever see those little Styrofoam packing peanuts used when sending fragile things in the mail? Most of the time those little packing peanuts are thrown away. Today we are going to recycle them to make a sculpture."

C. Packing Peanut Sculpture
1. Make animals, people, characters, sculptures.
2. Paint with small paint brushes or sharpie markers.
3. Share sculptures with the class.

CLOSURE/ DISCUSSION:

- What did you like most? Least?
- Was this easy or hard?
- What did you notice or learn about yourself today?

Facilitator Manual — Start Up!

WEEK 10

EXQUISITE CORPSE / PARTNER DRAWING

SELF PHASE

Purpose:
Physical Homeostasis

Goal:
Identity Formation/
Sensory Motor
Development

Neural Activity:
Cerebellum

Benefits:
- Community Building
- Development of Abstract Thinking
- Perceptual Development
- Development of Imagination

Duration:
12 Weeks

Session 1 - Monday

Activity: EXQUISITE CORPSE / PARTNER DRAWING
(A drawing game developed by artists in the early 1900's)

Art Materials:
- Markers
- Chalk Pastels
- 2 Pieces each of 9 x 12 paper

MUSIC FREEZE

BREATHING / MEDITATION
"Close your eyes or leave them open if you would like. Breathe in deeply through your nose or mouth, until your lungs are full. Let your breath out until your lungs are empty." Do this 3 times, or as many times as you are able."

ART DIRECTIVES:
A. Bi-Lateral Scribble:
   Two handed Marker drawing (1 Marker/crayon for each hand): Each movement is done for 9-10 seconds. We encourage the children to look at their marks on the paper, the teacher can stand at the front of the group and demonstrate on the chalkboard, describing the process of bilateral scribbling **(Younger children may need help with taping and movements at first):**
   1. Tape Paper onto table (horizontally).
   2. Make Random Marks with both hands.
   3. Make Vertical Lines beginning from the bottom of the paper to the top, up and down. (can alternate hands).
   4. Make Horizontal Lines, across paper with each hand on opposite edge of page," bringing their markers to meet in the middle. Have children cross the midline (cross arms to opposite sides of the paper and back to opposite side of page-repeat)
   5. Make two Arcs, or windshield wiper movements, back and forth. Let the Arcs move into two large circles and go around and around.
   6. Continue to make Circles in the reverse direction,- reverse again/ repeating.
   7. Make gentle Dots- now go up and down on the paper, now back and forth across the paper.
   8. Put one arm and hand over the other and make a Big X and now move the other arm and hand on top, now the other on top (repeat 4-5 times)
   9. Make Fast Circles, go around really fast, now gradually slower and smaller, until you have a small circle add dot in the middle of the smallest circle, and STOP.

Start Up!   Facilitator Manual

EXQUISITE CORPSE / PARTNER DRAWING

WEEK 10

B. Bi-Lateral Drawing:
Flip paper and re-tape paper to table
With markers in each hand children are instructed to:
1. Draw a starry sky
2. Draw some star people (can add cultural teachings about traditional star knowledge beliefs of particular population)
3. Draw a spaceship
4. Draw a moon

C. Scribble Chase
1. Select a partner (each child has 1 marker)
2. Determine who will be the leader, the follower
3. Say "GO" and the leader leads with the marker and the follower tries to follow the leader on the paper with their marker (30-40 seconds each turn)
4. Switch roles

MOTIVATION: "Who likes surprises? Today we are going to draw with partners. It's a game that artists used to play long ago where each person draws on the same paper but can't see what the other is drawing until the very end!"

D. Exquisite Corpse / Partner Drawing
1. Each child folds a piece of paper in half.
2. Each child starts drawing on his piece in one section of the folded paper, bringing the lines down slightly over the edge of the next section.
3. Partners trade papers when drawing in first section is complete.
4. Partner now has to continue drawing in second section from where the lines left off without looking at his partner's drawing.
5. Continue exchanging drawings for minutes.
6. ***Teacher:* emphasize the partnership- that you could not have made this art with out the other. How important it is to remember this partnership whenever the child is lonely, sad, scared, etc.**

CLOSURE/ DISCUSSION:

- What was it like to do the partner drawings?

- Having friends is important because?

- Whenever you feel sad, mad, etc you can think about a friend or tell a friend and feel better.

- What did you notice or learn about yourself today?

Facilitator Manual | Start Up! | 39

WEEK 10

SYMBOL OF PERSONAL POWER-STAMPING

SELF PHASE

Purpose:
Physical Homeostasis

Goal:
Identity Formation/
Sensory Motor
Development

Neural Activity:
Cerebellum

Benefits:
- Building Self- Esteem
- Learning adaptive coping strategies
- Identity Formation
- Development of Abstract Thinking
- Eye-hand Coordination
- Emotional Regulation
- Building Self Concept

Duration:
12 Weeks

Session 2 - Friday

ACTIVITY: SYMBOL OF PERSONAL POWER-STAMPING

Art Materials:
- Markers
- Pencil
- Small pieces of sponge
- Bowls of paint
- Largest paper for the desk space
- 3 Pieces each of 9 x 12 paper
- (Variation- Can do this on fabric and tie to wooden stick for a flag)

SIMON SAYS

BREATHING / MEDITATION
"Close your eyes and breathe deeply. Imagine you are walking alone in your favorite place in nature. You see something on the ground before you. You reach down and pick it up. It is a stone with a symbol on it. When you look at this symbol, it makes you feel strong and powerful, like you can handle any difficult situation which may arise. Look at this symbol as you hold it in your hand. It was given especially to you."

ART DIRECTIVES:
A. Bi-Lateral Scribble:
   Two handed Marker drawing (1 Marker/crayon for each hand): Each movement is done for 9-10 seconds. We encourage the children to look at their marks on the paper, the teacher can stand at the front of the group and demonstrate on the chalkboard, describing the process of bilateral scribbling **(Younger children may need help with taping and movements at first):**
   1. Tape Paper onto table (horizontally).
   2. Make Random Marks with both hands.
   3. Make Vertical Lines beginning from the bottom of the paper to the top, up and down. (can alternate hands).
   4. Make Horizontal Lines, across paper with each hand on opposite edge of page," bringing their markers to meet in the middle. Have children cross the midline (cross arms to opposite sides of the paper and back to opposite side of page-repeat)
   5. Make two Arcs, or windshield wiper movements, back and forth. Let the Arcs move into two large circles and go around and around.
   6. Continue to make Circles in the reverse direction,- reverse again/ repeating.

40   Start Up!   Facilitator Manual

SYMBOL OF PERSONAL POWER-STAMPING

WEEK 10

A. Bi-Lateral Scribble Cont.:
7. Make gentle Dots- now go up and down on the paper, now back and forth across the paper.
8. Put one arm and hand over the other and make a Big X and now move the other arm and hand on top, now the other on top (repeat 4-5 times)
9. Make Fast Circles, go around really fast, now gradually slower and smaller, until you have a small circle add dot in the middle of the smallest circle, and STOP.

B. Bi-Lateral Drawing:
Flip paper and re-tape paper to table
With markers in each hand children are instructed to:
1. Draw a groundline
2. Draw favorite animal
3. Draw tree
4. Draw a sun
5. Draw another animal of same type

MOTIVATION: "Does anyone know what a symbol is? A symbol is a shape or a design that represents something meaningful (give some examples of symbols form your culture and other cultures). A symbol is a shape or design that we look at and understand it's meaning instantly. Today you are going to design your own personal symbol that represents how powerful you are."

C. Symbol of Personal Power - Stamping
1. With pencil on large paper, each child sketches a symbol that gives them a sense of empowerment.
2. Children begin to fill in the symbol using sponge stamps dipped in different colors of paint.
3. **Teacher: Emphasize the symbol of personal power – this symbol is like your own personal flag to take home with you. Whenever you see this symbol you will feel strong.**
4. Share symbols with class.

CLOSURE/ DISCUSSION:

- What was it like to make your symbol?

- How does your symbol make you feel?

- Was it easy or hard?

- What did you notice or learn about yourself today?

WEEK 11

FOIL SELF SCULPTURES

SELF PHASE

Purpose:
Physical Homeostasis

Goal:
Identity Formation/
Sensory Motor
Development

Neural Activity:
Cerebellum

Benefits:
• Visual Perception
  Development
• Building Self
  Concept
• Building Self- Esteem
• Learning adaptive
  coping strategies
• Eye/Hand
  Coordination

Duration:
12 Weeks

Session 1 - Monday

ACTIVITY: FOIL SELF SCULPTURES

Art Materials:
• Markers
• Foil
• Masking Tape
• Largest paper for the desk space
• 3 Pieces each of 9 x 12 paper

HEAD SHOULDERS KNEES & TOES

BREATHING / MEDITATION
"Close your eyes and breathe deeply. Help your mind to rest and relax. Imagine yourself in a situation where people aren't acting kind towards you. Imagine that your feelings begin to be hurt. Now imagine you have a big mirror and you put it all around you; over the top of you; underneath you. Imagine you are inside this mirror, and all the unkindness is bouncing off the mirrors, unable to reach you. You understand that other's unkindness does not affect you."

ART DIRECTIVES:
A. Bi-Lateral Scribble:
   Two handed Marker drawing (1 Marker/crayon for each hand):
Each movement is done for 9-10 seconds. We encourage the children to look at their marks on the paper, the teacher can stand at the front of the group and demonstrate on the chalkboard, describing the process of bilateral scribbling **(Younger children may need help with taping and movements at first):**
   1. Tape Paper onto table (horizontally).
   2. Make Random Marks with both hands.
   3. Make Vertical Lines beginning from the bottom of the paper to the top, up and down. (can alternate hands).
   4. Make Horizontal Lines, across paper with each hand on opposite edge of page," bringing their markers to meet in the middle. Have children cross the midline (cross arms to opposite sides of the paper and back to opposite side of page-repeat)
   5. Make two Arcs, or windshield wiper movements, back and forth. Let the Arcs move into two large circles and go around and around.
   6. Continue to make Circles in the reverse direction,- reverse again/ repeating.

FOIL SELF SCULPTURES

WEEK 11

A. Bi-Lateral Scribble Cont.:
7. Make gentle Dots- now go up and down on the paper, now back and forth across the paper.
8. Put one arm and hand over the other and make a Big X and now move the other arm and hand on top, now the other on top (repeat 4-5 times)
9. Make Fast Circles, go around really fast, now gradually slower and smaller, until you have a small circle add dot in the middle of the smallest circle, and STOP.

B. Bi-Lateral Drawing:
Flip paper and re-tape paper to table
With markers in each hand children are instructed to:
1. Draw a groundline
2. Draw some flowers
3. Draw some worms
4. Draw some spiders
5. Draw some mosquitoes

MOTIVATION: "Who can think of some thing that foil looks like? (A mirror). Mirrors reflect things. If you hold a mirror up to the sun, it reflects sunlight. Today we are going to make sculptures of ourselves with tin foil, which reflects bad thoughts, bad words and bad feelings, so they can't get inside us and make us feel bad."

C. Foil Self-Sculptures
1. Roll foil in shapes of arms, legs, torso and head. Tape them together with masking tape.
2. Make shapes with foil for clothes. (Can make traditional dress according to culture: regalia, grass skirt, etc)
3. **Teacher: Emphasize that each child has the reflective power of a mirror to block out other people's bad thoughts, bad words, bad actions or bad feelings. Sometimes people we know say means things or do mean things and we can reflect these mean things like mirrors, and not let them into our bodies.**
4. Share sculptures with class.

CLOSURE/ DISCUSSION:

- What was it like to make a sculpture of yourself?

- How does your sculpture make you feel?

- Was it easy or hard?

- What did you notice or learn about yourself today?

Facilitator Manual — Start Up!

WEEK 11

NAME THAT DRAWING

SELF PHASE

Purpose:
Physical Homeostasis

Goal:
Identity Formation/
Sensory Motor
Development

Neural Activity:
Cerebellum

Benefits:
- Community Building
- Promotes Relaxation
- Perceptual Development
- Development of Imagination

Duration:
12 Weeks

Session 2 - Friday

ACTIVITY: NAME THAT DRAWING

Art Materials:
- Markers
- 3 Pieces each of 9 x 12 paper

MUSIC FREEZE

BREATHING / MEDITATION
"Close your eyes and breathe deeply. Imagine you are walking through a forest of big trees, following a stream of clear water. You come upon a clearing and see a giant waterfall. You jump into the water. It is refreshing and the perfect temperature for you. You swim to the waterfall and stand under it. You feel the cool water falling all over you. You suddenly hear the water speaking to you. It is telling you that it will heal you; removing all of your stress, worries, and loneliness that you carry. The water tells you that wherever you see water; in your sink, rivers, oceans, bathtub, or the water that you drink, that this is also part of the waterfall, and will continue to heal you. All you have to do is ask. You thank the waterfall and swim back to shore and walk back down the forest path. Gently open you eyes."

ART DIRECTIVES:
A. Bi-Lateral Scribble:
   Two handed Marker drawing (1 Marker/crayon for each hand):
Each movement is done for 9-10 seconds. We encourage the children to look at their marks on the paper, the teacher can stand at the front of the group and demonstrate on the chalkboard, describing the process of bilateral scribbling **(Younger children may need help with taping and movements at first):**
1. Tape Paper onto table (horizontally).
2. Make Random Marks with both hands.
3. Make Vertical Lines beginning from the bottom of the paper to the top, up and down. (can alternate hands).
4. Make Horizontal Lines, across paper with each hand on opposite edge of page," bringing their markers to meet in the middle. Have children cross the midline (cross arms to opposite sides of the paper and back to opposite side of page-repeat)
5. Make two Arcs, or windshield wiper movements, back and forth.
   Let the Arcs move into two large circles and go around and around.

Start Up! Facilitator Manual

NAME THAT DRAWING

WEEK 11

A. Bi-Lateral Scribble Cont.:
6. Continue to make Circles in the reverse direction,- reverse again/ repeating.
7. Make gentle Dots- now go up and down on the paper, now back and forth across the paper.
8. Put one arm and hand over the other and make a Big X and now move the other arm and hand on top, now the other on top (repeat 4-5 times)
9. Make Fast Circles, go around really fast, now gradually slower and smaller, until you have a small circle add dot in the middle of the smallest circle, and STOP.

B. Bi-Lateral Drawing:
Flip paper and re-tape paper to table
With markers in each hand children are instructed to:
1. Draw a groundline
2. Draw a cactus
3. Draw a desert
4. Draw a skull
5. Draw another cactus
6. Draw a coyote
7. Draw a moon

MOTIVATION: "Who likes to work with a partner? Today we are going to do something fun together."

C. Name that Drawing
1. Draw something on paper and the other guesses.
2. Take turns drawing people, places, things, heroes, super heroes, etc. and have the other guess.
3. Make them hard or easy.

CLOSURE/ DISCUSSION:

- What was it like to work with a partner?

- Was it easy or hard to guess what the other was drawing?

- What did you notice or learn about yourself today?

WEEK 12

FEELINGS SCULPTURES

SELF PHASE

Purpose:
Physical Homeostasis

Goal:
Identity Formation/
Sensory Motor
Development

Neural Activity:
Cerebellum

Benefits:
- Learning adaptive coping strategies
- Identity Formation
- Perceptual Development
- Emotional Development
- Emotional Recognition
- Emotional Regulation
- Emotional Containment
- Transforming negative to positive
- Experience of Control

Duration:
12 Weeks

Session 1 - Monday

ACTIVITY: FEELINGS SCULPTURES

Art Materials:
- Markers
- Popsicle sticks, balsa wood, foam, small boxes, scraps of things
- Tape 1" masking tape
- Construction paper
- Plaster gauze
- Water containers
- Bowl of Purifying Herbs (sage, copal, palo santo, tea leaves, etc)
- 3 Pieces each of 9 x 12 paper

SIMON SAYS

BREATHING / MEDITATION
"Close your eyes and breathe deeply. Feel your body heavy in the chair you are sitting in. Are there any places in your body that are holding onto any bad feelings? Imagine yourself as a tree with roots going deep into the earth until they come to an underground river. Imagine your roots are like a straw. Imagine sucking up this cool underground water from deep within the earth and bringing this water up into your tree body to wash away all the bad feelings. Imagine sucking up this healing water several times. When your bad feelings are washed away you can gently open your eyes."

ART DIRECTIVES:
A. Bi-Lateral Scribble:
   Two handed Marker drawing (1 Marker/crayon for each hand):
Each movement is done for 9-10 seconds. We encourage the children to look at their marks on the paper, the teacher can stand at the front of the group and demonstrate on the chalkboard, describing the process of bilateral scribbling **(Younger children may need help with taping and movements at first):**
   1. Tape Paper onto table (horizontally).
   2. Make Random Marks with both hands.
   3. Make Vertical Lines beginning from the bottom of the paper to the top, up and down. (can alternate hands).
   4. Make Horizontal Lines, across paper with each hand on opposite edge of page," bringing their markers to meet in the middle. Have children cross the midline (cross arms to opposite sides of the paper and back to opposite side of page-repeat)
   5. Make two Arcs, or windshield wiper movements, back and forth. Let the Arcs move into two large circles and go around and around.

46   Start Up!   Facilitator Manual

FEELINGS SCULPTURES   **WEEK 12**

A. Bi-Lateral Scribble Cont.:

6. Continue to make Circles in the reverse direction,- reverse again/ repeating.
7. Make gentle Dots- now go up and down on the paper, now back and forth across the paper.
8. Put one arm and hand over the other and make a Big X and now move the other arm and hand on top, now the other on top (repeat 4-5 times)
9. Make Fast Circles, go around really fast, now gradually slower and smaller, until you have a small circle add dot in the middle of the smallest circle, and STOP.

B. Bi-Lateral Drawing:

Flip paper and re-tape paper to table
With markers in each hand children are instructed to:

1. Draw a waterline
2. Draw a boat (can be a traditional boat of particular population and add cultural teachings)
3. Draw a motor or sails to the boat (if applicable)
4. Draw a flag (of particular people)
5. Draw someone fishing with a line in the water with a hook
6. Draw some fish in the water
7. Add a shark

MOTIVATION: "Who can name some good feelings? Who can name some bad feelings? Today we are going to do sculptures of a bad feeling. Think of a bad feeling and let it out into your sculpture, like we did when we made our clay bowls, remember? We will release these bad feelings so they are no longer in your body or your mind."

C. Feelings Sculptures

1. Construct a sculpture of a bad feeling using popsicle sticks, balsa wood, tea boxes, foam, scraps, tape and construction paper.
2. ***Teacher:* Emphasize that the child is releasing these feelings into their sculpture. They do not need to share what their feeling it is with anyone, just know it is moving out of them and into the materials.**
3. Teacher smudges all sculptures and says some prayers for all the bad feelings to be released from the sculptures and to go up with the smoke.
4. Cover sculpture with plaster gauze.
5. Ask if anyone would like to share.
6. Can paint sculptures at different time (after plaster is dry).

CLOSURE/ DISCUSSION:

- What was it like to make your sculpture?

- Was it easy or hard?

- What did you notice or learn about yourself today?

Facilitator Manual   Start Up!

WEEK 12

FEELINGS SCULPTURES, continued

SELF PHASE

Purpose:
Physical Homeostasis

Goal:
Identity Formation/
Sensory Motor
Development

Neural Activity:
Cerebellum

Benefits:
- Reinforcing positive emotions
- Emotional Recognition
- Emotional Regulation
- Visual/spatial perception
- Experience of Control

Duration:
12 Weeks

Session 2 - Friday

ACTIVITY: FEELINGS SCULPTURES, continued

Art Materials:
- Markers
- Popsicle sticks, balsa wood, foam, small boxes, scraps of things
- Tape 1" masking tape
- Construction paper
- Plaster gauze
- Water containers
- Bowl of Purifying Herbs (sage, copal, palo santo, tea leaves, etc)
- 3 Pieces each of 9 x 12 paper

HEAD SHOULDERS KNEES &TOES

BREATHING / MEDITATION
"Close your eyes. Imagine you are in a sweatlodge, kiva, church, or some ceremony that is practiced by your culture. Imagine feeling a deep spiritual connection to something very powerful and very big. You might call it God, Buddha, Wakan Tanka, Allah, or any number of names depending on which culture or religion you are from. Imagine this connection is full of love and happiness and this good feeling fills your body. Breathe deeply and feel the feeling of love and happiness."

ART DIRECTIVES:
A. Bi-Lateral Scribble:
   Two handed Marker drawing (1 Marker/crayon for each hand): Each movement is done for 9-10 seconds. We encourage the children to look at their marks on the paper, the teacher can stand at the front of the group and demonstrate on the chalkboard, describing the process of bilateral scribbling **(Younger children may need help with taping and movements at first):**
   1. Tape Paper onto table (horizontally).
   2. Make Random Marks with both hands.
   3. Make Vertical Lines beginning from the bottom of the paper to the top, up and down. (can alternate hands).
   4. Make Horizontal Lines, across paper with each hand on opposite edge of page," bringing their markers to meet in the middle. Have children cross the midline (cross arms to opposite sides of the paper and back to opposite side of page-repeat)
   5. Make two Arcs, or windshield wiper movements, back and forth. Let the Arcs move into two large circles and go around and around.
   6. Continue to make Circles in the reverse direction,- reverse again/ repeating.

FEELINGS SCULPTURES, continued

WEEK 12

A. Bi-Lateral Scribble Cont.:
7. Make gentle Dots- now go up and down on the paper, now back and forth across the paper.
8. Put one arm and hand over the other and make a Big X and now move the other arm and hand on top, now the other on top (repeat 4-5 times)
9. Make Fast Circles, go around really fast, now gradually slower and smaller, until you have a small circle add dot in the middle of the smallest circle, and STOP.

B. Bi-Lateral Drawing:
Flip paper and re-tape paper to table
With markers in each hand children are instructed to:
1. Draw a groundline
2. Draw a desert
3. Draw a cactus
4. Draw a tumbleweed
5. Draw a lizard
6. Draw a big rock
7. Draw a vulture in the sky

MOTIVATION: "Remember last time when we made sculptures out of a bunch of junk, and turned that junk into a beautiful sculpture about our bad feelings? What were some bad feelings? Who can name some good feelings? Today we are going to do sculptures of a good feeling. Think of a good feeling and let it out into your sculpture and let it into your body. This sculpture will hold this good feeling so it will stay with us even during hard times."

C. Feelings Sculptures
1. Construct a sculpture of a good feeling using popsicle sticks, balsa wood, tea boxes, foam, scraps, tape and construction paper.
2. **Teacher: Emphasize that the child is creating good feelings to put into their sculptures and their bodies. They do not need to share what their feeling is with anyone, unless they would like to. Let them know that this is their special sculpture to always make them feel good, even if you just think about it, you can get that good feeling to help you through hard times.**
3. Teacher smudges all sculptures and says some prayers for all the good feelings to stay with the children.
4. Cover sculpture with plaster gauze.
5. Ask if anyone would like to share.
6. Can paint sculptures at different time (after plaster is dry).

CLOSURE/ DISCUSSION:

- What was it like to make your sculpture?

- Was it easy or hard?

- What did you notice or learn about yourself today?

Facilitator Manual Start Up! 49

Congratulations!

You have completed the Self Phase, completing the first 12 weeks of START UP!

You can decide if your class is ready to move onto the Problem Phase section, or you can choose to start over in the Self Phase section. Remember: repetition creates, strengthens, and re-wires the brain's neural pathways, so it doesn't hurt to repeat activities.

Readiness to move to the Problem Phase is indicated by:

- Ability to engage in eye contact
- Ability to sit comfortably
- Ability and comfort in talking about art making
- Ability and comfort in talking about themselves
- Ability to admit that he/she is having problems
- Improvement of behavior at home and at school

THE PROBLEM PHASE - 12 weeks

The following activities are designed to offer children safe and enjoyable activities that will promote development.

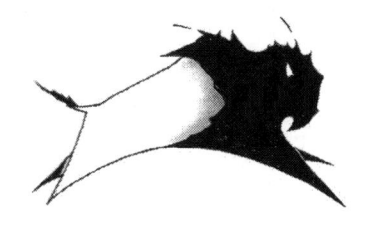

Objective

The Problem Phase is focused on emotions; the ability to identify, articulate, and regulate emotions. Emotional homeostasis is developed as a result of emotional exploration; building tolerance to a variety of emotions, while regulating and containing emotions simultaneously. Within a safe environment, children feel secure to non-verbally/verbally explore emotions through the carefully designed Start Up! art curriculum. Children are also allowed to develop preference (likes/ dislikes and priorities), through optional discussion/closure activity at the end of each session. Emotions are centered within the mid-brain, or limbic system of the brain.

Another goal of the Problem Phase is to build the mind-body self, a function of right hemisphere brain development (Schore, 2012). After the completion of the Self Phase in which physical homeostasis (body) is achieved, the Problem Phase is attuned to the emotions (mind), therefore creating a communication between mind-body.

The Problem Phase and the emotional homeostasis developed during this phase, is the building block to further self exploration, which will be presented and refined throughout the Transformation Phase and the Integration Phase of the Start Up! curriculum.

Many of the Sound/Movement activities, breathing/meditations, and bi-lateral scribble/ drawing activities are repeated throughout this curriculum. Repetition of activities is important to strengthen and reinforce new neural pathways. Repetition is also very beneficial for children as it creates predictability. When activities are predictable children can know what to expect thus, creating safety. Safety is vitally crucial in working with children and adolescents, especially those with traumatic backgrounds. It is important not to take children too deep too quickly. Start Up! slowly invites and engages children within a classroom, group or individual setting, to metaphorically explore, define, and refine sensory motor, emotional, cognitive and creative processes.

In The Problem Phase, we will explore emotions; learning to identify, articulate, regulate, contain positive and negative emotions within children and adolescents. The mid-brain, or the limbic brain is the brain's emotional center, therefore the Problem Phase activities will activate the limbic brain.

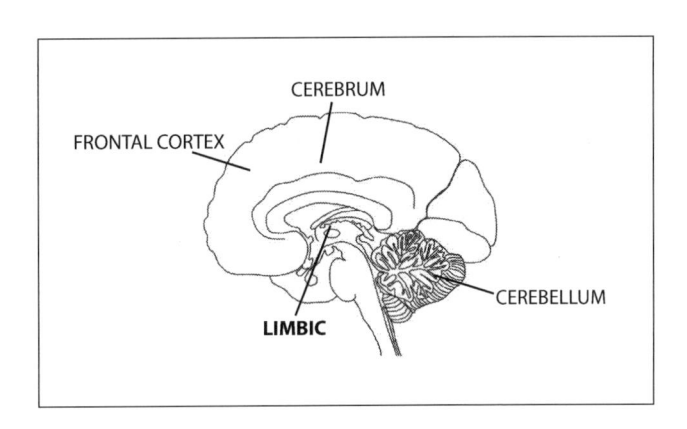

WEEK 1

INTRODUCTION COLLAGES

PROBLEM PHASE

Purpose:
Emotional Homeostasis

Goal:
Exploration of Feelings and Perceptions

Neural Activity:
Limbic

Benefits:
• Identity Formation
• Self Expression
• Experience of Control
• Decision Making

Duration:
12 Weeks

Session 1 - Monday

ACTIVITY: INTRODUCTION COLLAGES

Art Materials:
• Markers, (2 for each child)
• Largest paper for the desk space
• 3 Pieces each of 9x12 paper
• Magazines
• Scissors
• Gluesticks

SIMON SAYS

BREATHING / MEDITATION
"Breathe deeply, in and out slowly. Sit quietly. Meditate for a moment on what feels heavy to you; it may be difficult math homework, or your best friend is mad at you, or you are having a bad day. Imagine taking that heaviness off your shoulders and putting it on the floor next to you. You do not have to carry this. Notice how it feels to not carry it anymore. You do not have to pick it back up. I will pick it up for you."

ART DIRECTIVES:
A. Bi-Lateral Scribble:
   Two handed Marker drawing (1 Marker/crayon for each hand):
Each movement is done for 9-10 seconds. We encourage the children to look at their marks on the paper, the teacher can stand at the front of the group and demonstrate on the chalkboard, describing the process of bilateral scribbling **(Younger children may need help with taping and movements at first):**
   1. Tape Paper onto table (horizontally).
   2. Make Random Marks with both hands.
   3. Make Vertical Lines beginning from the bottom of the paper to the top, up and down. (can alternate hands).
   4. Make Horizontal Lines, across paper with each hand on opposite edge of page," bringing their markers to meet in the middle. Have children cross the midline (cross arms to opposite sides of the paper and back to opposite side of page-repeat)
   5. Make two Arcs, or windshield wiper movements, back and forth. Let the Arcs move into two large circles and go around and around.

---

52 · Start Up! · Facilitator Manual

INTRODUCTION COLLAGES

WEEK 1

A. Bi-Lateral Scribble Cont.:
6. Continue to make Circles in the reverse direction,- reverse again/ repeating.
7. Make gentle Dots- now go up and down on the paper, now back and forth across the paper.
8. Put one arm and hand over the other and make a Big X and now move the other arm and hand on top, now the other on top (repeat 4-5 times)
9. Make Fast Circles, go around really fast, now gradually slower and smaller, until you have a small circle add dot in the middle of the smallest circle, and STOP.

B. Bi-Lateral Drawing:
Flip paper and re-tape paper to table
With markers in each hand children are instructed to:
1. Draw a groundline
2. Draw a house with windows and door (tipi, wigwam, hut, traditional home, can add cultural teachings about traditional homes of particular population)
3. Draw a tree
4. Draw a basket of apples underneath the tree (or can be traditional food and add cultural teachings about the traditional foods of particular population)
5. Put clouds up in the sky
6. Sun / Birds

MOTIVATION: "A great way to learn about themselves, and exercise control over own privacy as they can tell what they want to tell about themselves. "Pretend we are all strangers. Today we are going to introduce ourselves sharing with the others what you want us to know about you……you can include your Tribe, your beliefs, values, hobbies, etc."

C. Introduction Collages:
1. Fold paper in half like a greeting card.
2. Children can cut out images which symbolize things they would like you to know about themselves and glue on outside of card.
3. On inside of card glue images which symbolize things they may not tell others about themselves.
4. Pick 3 favorite images that most describe you.

CLOSURE/ DISCUSSION

- What image did you like best, least?

- What did you focus on most?

- Are there images repeated in your image?

- What did you notice or learn about yourself today?

Facilitator Manual Start Up!

WEEK 1

MAGIC CARPET RIDE

PROBLEM PHASE

Purpose:
Emotional Homeostasis

Goal:
Exploration of Feelings and Perceptions

Neural Activity:
Limbic

Benefits:
- Development of Imagination
- Promotes Abstract Thinking
- Expression of Self
- Identity Formation

Duration:
12 Weeks

Session 2 - Friday

ACTIVITY: MAGIC CARPET RIDE

Art Materials:
- Markers,
- Largest paper for the desk space
- 3 Pieces each of 9 x 12 paper
- Pastels
- Colored pencils

HEAD/SHOULDER/KNEES & TOES

BREATHING / MEDITATION
"Breathe deeply, in and out slowly. Meditate for a moment that all worries, stress and chaos, is like a ball of string in your mind. Imagine putting that ball of string into a balloon, and letting it go. See it floating up into the air and disappearing into the sky. How does this feel in your body, and in your mind."

ART DIRECTIVES:
A. Bi-Lateral Scribble:
　Two handed Marker drawing (1 Marker/crayon for each hand):
Each movement is done for 9-10 seconds. We encourage the children to look at their marks on the paper, the teacher can stand at the front of the group and demonstrate on the chalkboard, describing the process of bilateral scribbling **(Younger children may need help with taping and movements at first):**
　1. Tape Paper onto table (horizontally).
　2. Make Random Marks with both hands.
　3. Make Vertical Lines beginning from the bottom of the paper to the top, up and down. (can alternate hands).
　4. Make Horizontal Lines, across paper with each hand on opposite edge of page," bringing their markers to meet in the middle. Have children cross the midline (cross arms to opposite sides of the paper and back to opposite side of page-repeat)
　5. Make two Arcs, or windshield wiper movements, back and forth. Let the Arcs move into two large circles and go around and around.
　6. Continue to make Circles in the reverse direction,- reverse again/ repeating.

MAGIC CARPET RIDE

WEEK 1

A. Bi-Lateral Scribble Cont.:
7. Make gentle Dots- now go up and down on the paper, now back and forth across the paper.
8. Put one arm and hand over the other and make a Big X and now move the other arm and hand on top, now the other on top (repeat 4-5 times)
9. Make Fast Circles, go around really fast, now gradually slower and smaller, until you have a small circle add dot in the middle of the smallest circle, and STOP.

B. Bi-Lateral Drawing:
Flip paper and re-tape paper to table
With markers in each hand children are instructed to:
1. Draw a starry sky
2. Draw some star people (can add cultural teachings about traditional star knowledge beliefs of particular population)
3. Draw a spaceship
4. Draw a moon

C. Scribble Chase
1. Select a partner (each child has 1 marker)
2. Determine who will be the leader, the follower
3. Say "GO" and the leader leads with the marker and the follower tries to follow the leader on the paper with their marker (30-40 seconds each turn)
4. Switch roles

MOTIVATION: "Use your imagination…Today we are going on a ride on a magic carpet. It will take you anywhere you want to go… where would you go?"

D. Magic Carpet Ride
1. Have children close their eyes, and sit straight in their chairs. (You can play soft music in the background)
2. Imagine you are sitting on a fluffy cozy carpet outside.
3. You can see the blue sky, the sun and the clouds.
4. Suddenly the carpet lifts off the ground and you are gently are carried through the sky to wherever you wish to go.
5. Where are you going? (Let some time pass, while listening to the music)
6. Now you are brought back to where you began, and are lowered back to the earth.
7. Gently open your eyes.
8. Draw where you went on your magic carpet ride.

CLOSURE/ DISCUSSION

- Where did you go?

- Can you tell me one feeling you had while you were there?

- What did you like best, least?

- What did you notice or learn about yourself today?

Facilitator Manual Start Up!

WEEK 2

TREASURE BOX DELIVERY

PROBLEM PHASE

Purpose:
Emotional Homeostasis

Goal:
Exploration of Feelings and Perceptions

Neural Activity:
Limbic

Benefits:
- Development of Imagination
- Emotional Development
- Abstract Thinking
- Identity Formation

Duration:
12 Weeks

Session 1 - Monday

ACTIVITY: TREASURE BOX DELIVERY

Art Materials:
- Markers
- Largest paper for the desk space
- 2 Pieces of 9x12 paper
- Oil Pastels
- Colored Pencils

MUSIC FREEZE

BREATHING / MEDITATION
"Close your eyes and breathe deeply. Imagine you are at the ocean. You see a box floating on the water. It reaches the shore and you pick it up and open it. Inside is a golden key. Immediately you know that this key is to help you solve any problem you may have. Think of a problem you might have in your life and imagine asking the key to help you solve it. Sometimes the answer might take awhile to appear and sometimes it might appear quickly. Imagine receiving an answer to your problem quickly. Thank the golden key and gently open your eyes."

ART DIRECTIVES:
A. Bi-Lateral Scribble:
   Two handed Marker drawing (1 Marker/crayon for each hand): Each movement is done for 9-10 seconds. We encourage the children to look at their marks on the paper, the teacher can stand at the front of the group and demonstrate on the chalkboard, describing the process of bilateral scribbling **(Younger children may need help with taping and movements at first):**
1. Tape Paper onto table (horizontally).
2. Make Random Marks with both hands.
3. Make Vertical Lines beginning from the bottom of the paper to the top, up and down. (can alternate hands).
4. Make Horizontal Lines, across paper with each hand on opposite edge of page," bringing their markers to meet in the middle. Have children cross the midline (cross arms to opposite sides of the paper and back to opposite side of page-repeat)
5. Make two Arcs, or windshield wiper movements, back and forth. Let the Arcs move into two large circles and go around and around.
6. Continue to make Circles in the reverse direction,- reverse again/ repeating.

Start Up! Facilitator Manual

TREASURE BOX DELIVERY

WEEK 2

A. Bi-Lateral Scribble Cont.:
7. Make gentle Dots- now go up and down on the paper, now back and forth across the paper.
8. Put one arm and hand over the other and make a Big X and now move the other arm and hand on top, now the other on top (repeat 4-5 times)
9. Make Fast Circles, go around really fast, now gradually slower and smaller, until you have a small circle add dot in the middle of the smallest circle, and STOP.

B. Bi-Lateral Drawing:
Flip paper and re-tape paper to table
With markers in each hand children are instructed to:
1. Draw a waterline
2. Draw a boat (can be a traditional boat of particular population and add cultural teachings)
3. Draw a motor or sails to the boat (if applicable)
4. Draw a flag
5. Draw someone fishing with a line in the water with a hook
6. Draw some fish in the water
7. Add a shark
8. Draw a starfish in the water
9. Add clouds/sun/birds
10. TEACHER- If you are a people originated near water, include cultural traditions and stories of water.

MOTIVATION: "Today we are going to pretend that a box was delivered to you, that is just for you. Inside is what exactly what you have always wanted more than anything."

C. Treasure Box Delivery
1. Close your eyes and imagine what your box looks like.
2. Inside is exactly what you have always wanted.
3. It can be an object, or many objects, place, a person, an idea, etc
4. Is it big, is it small?
5. Pay attention to the feelings you are experiencing.
6. Draw what was inside the box.

CLOSURE/ DISCUSSION

- Can you tell me one feeling you would have if you got that present?

- What was hard, easy?

- What did you learn about yourself today?

Facilitator Manual — Start Up!

WEEK 2

SEEING YOUR FUTURE

PROBLEM PHASE

Purpose:
Emotional Homeostasis

Goal:
Exploration of Feelings and Perceptions

Neural Activity:
Limbic

Benefits:
- Development of Hope
- Opportunity for Choices
- Develop Abstract Thinking

Duration:
12 Weeks

Session 2 - Friday

ACTIVITY: SEEING YOUR FUTURE

Art Materials:
- Markers
- Largest paper for the desk space
- 2 Pieces of 9x12 paper
- Oil Pastels
- Colored Pencils

SIMON SAYS

BREATHING / MEDITATION
"Close your eyes and breathe deeply. Imagine yourself standing at the top of a mountain. You feel the cool wind blowing by. You are thinking about your life and thinking about your future. You may have a big decision to make coming up, like what school to go to, or if you should try out for a sports team. Or it may be a decision you need to make in the distant future, like what you want to be when you grow up, etc. Imagine a relative you once knew who has passed away, or an ancestor who passed away before you met them. Imagine seeing their spirit descend from the clouds above. Imagine asking your relative or ancestor for guidance in your big decision. What does this spirit tell you? Express your gratitude to this spirit and gently open your eyes."

ART DIRECTIVES:
A. Bi-Lateral Scribble:
   Two handed Marker drawing (1 Marker/crayon for each hand): Each movement is done for 9-10 seconds. We encourage the children to look at their marks on the paper, the teacher can stand at the front of the group and demonstrate on the chalkboard, describing the process of bilateral scribbling **(Younger children may need help with taping and movements at first):**
  1. Tape Paper onto table (horizontally).
  2. Make Random Marks with both hands.
  3. Make Vertical Lines beginning from the bottom of the paper to the top, up and down. (can alternate hands).
  4. Make Horizontal Lines, across paper with each hand on opposite edge of page," bringing their markers to meet in the middle. Have children cross the midline (cross arms to opposite sides of the paper and back to opposite side of page-repeat)
  5. Make two Arcs, or windshield wiper movements, back and forth. Let the Arcs move into two large circles and go around and around.
  6. Continue to make Circles in the reverse direction,- reverse again/ repeating.
  7. Make gentle Dots- now go up and down on the paper, now back and forth across the paper.

SEEING YOUR FUTURE — WEEK 2

A. Bi-Lateral Scribble Cont.:
8. Put one arm and hand over the other and make a Big X and now move the other arm and hand on top, now the other on top (repeat 4-5 times)
9. Make Fast Circles, go around really fast, now gradually slower and smaller, until you have a small circle add dot in the middle of the smallest circle, and STOP.

B. Bi-Lateral Drawing:
Flip paper and re-tape paper to table.
With markers in each hand children are instructed to:
1. Draw underground
2. Draw a snake underground
3. Draw a family of snakes underground
4. Draw a prairie dog underground
5. Draw a fox
6. Draw a rabbit
7. Add a family of rabbits
8. Draw some ants
9. Add clouds/sun/birds above ground

MOTIVATION: : "Who remembers what we did before? Recall magic carpet ride, and the box delivery? I would like you to use your imagination to look to your future. What do you feel you were put on this planet to do? What is your life's work? Sittingbull and Crazyhorse were famous leaders of the Native Americans, Billy Mills was the first Native American to win an Olympic gold medal, Rosa Parks and Martin Luther King were famous civil rights leaders for the African Americans, Cesar Chavez and Pancho Villa were famous leaders for the Latino. Today we are going to imagine what our future is and our life's purpose in it."

C. Seeing Your Future
1. Close your eyes and think of yourself as a child, teen, and adult.
2. Imagine what you might look like.
3. Imagine yourself doing important work in your life.
4. What is this important work that you might do? It might be that you are a doctor curing diseases, or a lawyer protecting your people, or a researcher, helping others, etc. What is your important life's work?
5. Can play soft traditional music in background.
6. Open your eyes and draw what you saw for your life's work.
7. *Teacher:* " **You can do anything you want to do in life. You can do your life's work. You need to believe in yourself. You just need to work at it and I am here to support you."** Encourage children to think about their futures and life's work whenever they feel down, or if someone tells them they can't do something.

CLOSURE/ DISCUSSION

- Can you tell me one feeling you would have if you were in that life's work?

- Was this easy or hard?

- What did you learn about yourself today?

WEEK 3

WHO ARE YOU?

PROBLEM PHASE

Purpose:
Emotional Homeostasis

Goal:
Exploration of Feelings and Perceptions

Neural Activity:
Limbic

Benefits:
• Increase in Critical Thinking
• Identity Formation
• Emotional Regulation

Duration:
12 Weeks

Session 1 - Monday

ACTIVITY: WHO ARE YOU?

Art Materials:
• Markers
• Largest paper for the desk space
• 2 Pieces each of 9x12 paper
• Construction Paper
• Glue

HEAD SHOULDERS KNEES AND TOES

BREATHING / MEDITATION
"Close your eyes and breathe deeply. Imagine yourself as you are now. Think about all the experiences you have had in your life; both rewarding and challenging. Think about how these experiences that are unique to you have helped you learn valuable lessons, which will help you be strong and brave throughout your life. Imagine taking the positive qualities that you have developed within yourself as a result of these experiences, and using them as a powerful force to help you accomplish your goals. You do not have to feel defeated or a victim. Feel yourself strong and powerful because of these experiences and imagine yourself accomplishing one goal for yourself."

ART DIRECTIVES:
A. Bi-Lateral Scribble:
   Two handed Marker drawing (1 Marker/crayon for each hand): Each movement is done for 9-10 seconds. We encourage the children to look at their marks on the paper, the teacher can stand at the front of the group and demonstrate on the chalkboard, describing the process of bilateral scribbling (**Younger children may need help with taping and movements at first**):
  1. Tape Paper onto table (horizontally).
  2. Make Random Marks with both hands.
  3. Make Vertical Lines beginning from the bottom of the paper to the top, up and down. (can alternate hands).
  4. Make Horizontal Lines, across paper with each hand on opposite edge of page," bringing their markers to meet in the middle. Have children cross the midline (cross arms to opposite sides of the paper and back to opposite side of page-repeat)
  5. Make two Arcs, or windshield wiper movements, back and forth. Let the Arcs move into two large circles and go around and around.

Start Up! Facilitator Manual

WHO ARE YOU?

WEEK 3

A. Bi-Lateral Scribble Cont.:
6. Continue to make Circles in the reverse direction,- reverse again/ repeating.
7. Make gentle Dots- now go up and down on the paper, now back and forth across the paper.
8. Put one arm and hand over the other and make a Big X and now move the other arm and hand on top, now the other on top (repeat 4-5 times)
9. Make Fast Circles, go around really fast, now gradually slower and smaller, until you have a small circle add dot in the middle of the smallest circle, and STOP.

B. Bi-Lateral Drawing:
Flip paper and re-tape paper to table
With markers in each hand children are instructed to:
1. Draw a groundline
2. Draw a dinosaur (or animal special to traditions of particular population, buffalo, whale, jaguar, etc. Include cultural teachings of animal)
3. Draw tree
4. Draw a sun
5. Draw another animal

MOTIVATION: "Have you ever thought about who you really are? Who are you and what good qualities do you have? Think about all the good things about yourself. Nobody is perfect, not one single person on this earth is perfect, even all the leaders we talked about last week weren't perfect. We all have challenges and that is ok. It gives us something to work on, as humans. Think about what might be a challenging quality you have about yourself."

C. Who are you?
1. Fold paper in half to make a crease in the middle
2. Who are you? What are your positive qualities?
3. What are your challenging qualities?
4. Cut out symbols with construction paper that represent challenging qualities and glue them on one side of the paper
5. Cut out symbols with construction paper that represent positive qualities and glue them on the opposite side of the paper.

CLOSURE/ DISCUSSION

- "What is your favorite positive quality about yourself?"

- "What is something you want to work on?"

- "What did you learn about yourself today?"

WEEK 3

LEADER OR BULLY?

PROBLEM PHASE

Purpose:
Emotional Homeostasis

Goal:
Exploration of Feelings and Perceptions

Neural Activity:
Limbic

Benefits:
• Development of Critical Thinking
• Development of Social skills
• Community Building
• Identity Formation

Duration:
12 Weeks

Session 2 - Friday

ACTIVITY: LEADER OR BULLY?

Art Materials:
• Markers
• Largest paper for the desk space
• 3 Pieces each of 9x12 paper
• Large craft paper
• Gluesticks

MUSIC FREEZE

BREATHING / MEDITATION
"Close your eyes and breathe deeply. Imagine you are in the hallway at school. You see a crowd of kids causing a commotion. You walk towards the crowd to see a small child getting bullied by a group of older kids. The child is on the floor of the hallway, crying while the other kids continue to tease and call the child names, while laughing. You know this is wrong and you know you must stop this immediately. What do you do? What do you say to stop this mistreatment of a fellow student? Imagine how you would act in this situation."

ART DIRECTIVES:
A. Bi-Lateral Scribble:
  Two handed Marker drawing (1 Marker/crayon for each hand): Each movement is done for 9-10 seconds. We encourage the children to look at their marks on the paper, the teacher can stand at the front of the group and demonstrate on the chalkboard, describing the process of bilateral scribbling **(Younger children may need help with taping and movements at first):**
  1. Tape Paper onto table (horizontally).
  2. Make Random Marks with both hands.
  3. Make Vertical Lines beginning from the bottom of the paper to the top, up and down. (can alternate hands).
  4. Make Horizontal Lines, across paper with each hand on opposite edge of page," bringing their markers to meet in the middle. Have children cross the midline (cross arms to opposite sides of the paper and back to opposite side of page-repeat)
  5. Make two Arcs, or windshield wiper movements, back and forth. Let the Arcs move into two large circles and go around and around.
  6. Continue to make Circles in the reverse direction,- reverse again/ repeating.
  7. Make gentle Dots- now go up and down on the paper, now back and forth across the paper.

Start Up!   Facilitator Manual

LEADER OR BULLY?   WEEK 3

A. Bi-Lateral Scribble Cont.:
8. Put one arm and hand over the other and make a Big X and now move the other arm and hand on top, now the other on top (repeat 4-5 times)
9. Make Fast Circles, go around really fast, now gradually slower and smaller, until you have a small circle add dot in the middle of the smallest circle, and STOP.

B. Bi-Lateral Drawing:
Flip paper and re-tape paper to table
With markers in each hand children are instructed to:
1. Draw a groundline
2. Draw a desert
3. Draw a cactus
4. Draw a tumbleweed
5. Draw a lizard
6. Draw a big rock
7. Draw a vulture in the sky
8. Teacher- You can include traditions and stories of Desert Tribes; diet, how they obtained water, etc.

MOTIVATION: "Have you known a bully in your life? A bully forces people to do things, a leader inspires and supports others to do their best. Bullies can be kids, and they can be adults. Bullying can happen at school, at work, at home, or around town."

C. Bully or Leader
1. Hang a large piece of butcher or craft paper on the wall.
2. Draw a line down the middle of the paper. Label one side "Bully" and other side "Leader"
3. Have children draw symbols of what it takes to be a **bully** on a piece of paper at their desks.
4. Have children draw symbols of what it takes to be a **leader** on a piece of paper at their desks.
5. Children will then cut the "bully" symbols out and glue them to the craft paper on the side marked "Bully"
6. Children will then cut the "leader" symbols out and glue them to the craft paper on the side marked "Leader"
7. *Teacher:* **Explain how we are all equal and should live in harmony with each other. Explain that if you or anyone you know is being bullied to report it to you, or another adult. Encourage children to anonymously report bullying by leaving a note on a special locked box on your desk. Bullying has a causal relationship with suicide, and is the second leading cause of death in children 10-24 years old.**

CLOSURE/ DISCUSSION

- What did you learn about bullies today?
- What did you learn about leaders today?
- What did you learn about yourself today?

WEEK 4 — DRAW A BRIDGE

PROBLEM PHASE

Purpose:
Emotional Homeostasis

Goal:
Exploration of Feelings and Perceptions

Neural Activity:
Limbic

Benefits:
- Installation of Hope
- Identity Formation
- Acknowledging the Past
- Emotional Regulation

Duration:
12 Weeks

Session 1 - Monday

ACTIVITY: DRAW A BRIDGE

Art Materials:
- Markers
- Largest paper for the desk space
- 2 Pieces each of 9x12 paper
- Oil Pastels

SIMON SAYS

BREATHING / MEDITATION
"Close your eyes and breathe deeply. Think about the things you have experienced in your life. Think about the good experiences and the difficult experiences in your past. What are some good experiences you want to have in your future? You may want to go to college and work towards becoming a doctor, lawyer, firefighter, nurse, or veterinarian, etc. You may want to travel or do both. Imagine your future and what you want in it. Take some slow deep breaths here and then gently open your eyes."

ART DIRECTIVES:
A. Bi-Lateral Scribble:
　　Two handed Marker drawing (1 Marker/crayon for each hand): Each movement is done for 9-10 seconds. We encourage the children to look at their marks on the paper, the teacher can stand at the front of the group and demonstrate on the chalkboard, describing the process of bilateral scribbling **(Younger children may need help with taping and movements at first):**
  1. Tape Paper onto table (horizontally).
  2. Make Random Marks with both hands.
  3. Make Vertical Lines beginning from the bottom of the paper to the top, up and down. (can alternate hands).
  4. Make Horizontal Lines, across paper with each hand on opposite edge of page," bringing their markers to meet in the middle. Have children cross the midline (cross arms to opposite sides of the paper and back to opposite side of page-repeat)
  5. Make two Arcs, or windshield wiper movements, back and forth. Let the Arcs move into two large circles and go around and around.
  6. Continue to make Circles in the reverse direction,- reverse again/ repeating.

Start Up!

DRAW A BRIDGE

WEEK 4

A. Bi-Lateral Scribble Cont.:
7. Make gentle Dots- now go up and down on the paper, now back and forth across the paper.
8. Put one arm and hand over the other and make a Big X and now move the other arm and hand on top, now the other on top (repeat 4-5 times)
9. Make Fast Circles, go around really fast, now gradually slower and smaller, until you have a small circle add dot in the middle of the smallest circle, and STOP.

B. Bi-Lateral Drawing:
Flip paper and re-tape paper to table
With markers in each hand children are instructed to:
1. Draw a groundline
2. Draw favorite animal
3. Draw tree
4. Draw a sun
5. Draw another animal of same type

MOTIVATION: "Bridges help us cross from one body of land to another so we can get to where we are going. There are many famous bridges throughout the world: (have children name some bridges of the world and local bridges too). Today we are going to draw a bridge."

C. Draw a Bridge
Teacher: **You can talk about the ways each culture would cross a body of water and what an old style of bridge would look like. Children can choose to draw a bridge similar to what their ancestors used.**
1. Turn your paper horizontally on your desk.
2. Draw a bridge from one side of the paper to the other.
3. On the left side of the bridge draw where you were in the past.
4. On the right side of the bridge draw where you are going in your future (your goals of your future).
5. Somewhere on the bridge draw yourself where you are right now (where you think you are in relation to your past and future).

CLOSURE/ DISCUSSION

- Where did you start and where are you headed?

- Where are you on the bridge?

- What did you learn about yourself today?

Facilitator Manual — Start Up! — 65

WEEK 4

MULTI-MEDIA ART PROJECT-DRAW YOUR INITIALS

PROBLEM PHASE

Purpose:
Emotional Homeostasis

Goal:
Exploration of Feelings and Perceptions

Neural Activity:
Limbic

Benefits:
- Self Recognition
- Identity Formation
- Exploring Preferences

Duration:
12 Weeks

Session 2 - Friday

ACTIVITY: MULTI-MEDIA ART PROJECT-DRAW YOUR INITIALS

Art Materials:
- Markers, (2 for each child)
- 2 Pieces each of 9x12 paper
- Oil pastels
- Chalk pastels
- Acrylic paint

HEAD SHOULDERS KNEES & TOES

BREATHING / MEDITATION
"Close your eyes or leave them open if you really need to. Breathe in deeply through your nose or mouth, until your lungs are full. Let your breath out until your lungs are empty." Do this 3 times, or as many times as tolerated. Can set a timer for longer and longer times, up to 3-5 minutes.

ART DIRECTIVES:
A. Bi-Lateral Scribble:
   Two handed Marker drawing (1 Marker/crayon for each hand): Each movement is done for 9-10 seconds. We encourage the children to look at their marks on the paper, the teacher can stand at the front of the group and demonstrate on the chalkboard, describing the process of bilateral scribbling **(Younger children may need help with taping and movements at first):**
   1. Tape Paper onto table (horizontally).
   2. Make Random Marks with both hands.
   3. Make Vertical Lines beginning from the bottom of the paper to the top, up and down. (can alternate hands).
   4. Make Horizontal Lines, across paper with each hand on opposite edge of page," bringing their markers to meet in the middle. Have children cross the midline (cross arms to opposite sides of the paper and back to opposite side of page-repeat)
   5. Make two Arcs, or windshield wiper movements, back and forth. Let the Arcs move into two large circles and go around and around.

66   Start Up!   Facilitator Manual

MULTI-MEDIA ART PROJECT-DRAW YOUR INITIALS

WEEK 4

A. Bi-Lateral Scribble Cont.:
6. Continue to make Circles in the reverse direction,- reverse again/ repeating.
7. Make gentle Dots- now go up and down on the paper, now back and forth across the paper.
8. Put one arm and hand over the other and make a Big X and now move the other arm and hand on top, now the other on top (repeat 4-5 times)
9. Make Fast Circles, go around really fast, now gradually slower and smaller, until you have a small circle add dot in the middle of the smallest circle, and STOP.

B. Bi-Lateral Drawing:
Flip paper and re-tape paper to table
With markers in each hand children are instructed to:
1. Draw a sky
2. Draw a moon
3. Draw stars
4. Draw planets
5. Draw a spaceship
6. Draw a star being (alien)

MOTIVATION: To get comfortable with different art media. To move from structured media to unstructured media to elicit emotion. To develop a preference for one medium over another and express the preference. "Different art materials make us feel different ways….today we are going to work with different art materials and we are going to see how each one makes us feel."

C. Draw your Initials
1. Scribble intials with marker, with one hand, decorate with markers only, for 5 minutes
2. Now switch to oil pastels- decorate initials for 5 minutes
3. Chalk Pastels- 5 minutes
4. Paint- 5-10 minutes

CLOSURE/ DISCUSSION

- What media did you like the best, least?
- Which initial do you like best?
- What did you notice about yourself pertaining to your name?
- Is there anything you noticed that surprised you?

Facilitator Manual   Start Up!

WEEK 5   THE BEST THING I COULD BE / THE WORST THING I COULD BE

PROBLEM PHASE

Purpose:
Emotional Homeostasis

Goal:
Exploration of Feelings and Perceptions

Neural Activity:
Limbic

Benefits:
- Development of Abstract Thinking
- Promotes Critical Thinking
- Prevention

Duration:
12 Weeks

Session 1 - Monday

ACTIVITY: THE BEST THING I COULD BE / THE WORST THING I COULD BE

Art Materials:
- Markers
- 2 Pieces each of 9x12 paper
- Oil Pastels

HEAD SHOULDERS KNEES &TOES

BREATHING / MEDITATION
"Close your eyes and breathe deeply. Think about someone who you do or do not know, someone famous, or not famous, who has done great things to help the world, the people, or animals, etc. Imagine yourself doing something really great and impactful in the world. Imagine creating the best person you could possibly be."

ART DIRECTIVES:
A. Bi-Lateral Scribble:
    Two handed Marker drawing (1 Marker/crayon for each hand): Each movement is done for 9-10 seconds. We encourage the children to look at their marks on the paper, the teacher can stand at the front of the group and demonstrate on the chalkboard, describing the process of bilateral scribbling **(Younger children may need help with taping and movements at first):**
1. Tape Paper onto table (horizontally).
2. Make Random Marks with both hands.
3. Make Vertical Lines beginning from the bottom of the paper to the top, up and down. (can alternate hands).
4. Make Horizontal Lines, across paper with each hand on opposite edge of page," bringing their markers to meet in the middle. Have children cross the midline (cross arms to opposite sides of the paper and back to opposite side of page-repeat)
5. Make two Arcs, or windshield wiper movements, back and forth. Let the Arcs move into two large circles and go around and around.

68   Start Up!   Facilitator Manual

THE BEST THING I COULD BE / THE WORST THING I COULD BE

WEEK 5

A. Bi-Lateral Scribble Cont.:
6. Continue to make Circles in the reverse direction,- reverse again/ repeating.
7. Make gentle Dots- now go up and down on the paper, now back and forth across the paper.
8. Put one arm and hand over the other and make a Big X and now move the other arm and hand on top, now the other on top (repeat 4-5 times)
9. Make Fast Circles, go around really fast, now gradually slower and smaller, until you have a small circle add dot in the middle of the smallest circle, and STOP.

B. Bi-Lateral Drawing:
Flip paper and re-tape paper to table
With markers in each hand children are instructed to:
1. Draw a ground line
2. Draw a jungle of trees
3. Draw a monkey
4. Draw a tiger
5. Draw a river
6. Draw a parrot
7. Draw fish in the river

MOTIVATION: "Think about who you would like to be, the best possible person you could ever be. Think about the worst person you could ever be and what that would be like."

C. The Best Thing I Could Be / The Worst Thing I Could Be
1. Put paper horizontally onto desk and draw a line down the middle.
2. Label the left section "The Best Person I Could Be" and in the right section, "The Worst Person I Could Be."
3. Draw with oil pastels: figures, symbols or shapes which represent the Best Self/Worst Self in the appropriate sections of the paper.

CLOSURE/ DISCUSSION

- What is the best/ worst thing you could be?

- Is it new or did you have to think about it?

- What would be the consequences of being the best/worst thing?

WEEK 5

ACTING IN A FEELING / ACTING OUT A FEELING

PROBLEM PHASE

Purpose:
Emotional Homeostasis

Goal:
Exploration of Feelings and Perceptions

Neural Activity:
Limbic

Benefits:
- Emotional Development
- Emotional Regulation
- Emotional Recognition
- Emotional Expression
- Learning Adaptive Coping Strategies

Duration:
12 Weeks

Session 2 - Friday

ACTIVITY: ACTING IN A FEELING / ACTING OUT A FEELING

Art Materials:
- Markers
- 2 Pieces, largest paper for the desk space
- Oil Pastels

MUSIC FREEZE

BREATHING / MEDITATION
"Close your eyes and breathe deeply. Imagine feeling a difficult feeling. It could be angry, sad, lonely, etc. This feeling does not feel good. Imagine how you normally act when you feel this feeling…you might cry, yell, throw things, hit a sibling, etc. Imagine that you had complete control over how you act when you are feeling this way. Imagine how would you choose to act instead? Breathe deeply while imagining a different way of acting out this difficult feeling."

ART DIRECTIVES:
A. Bi-Lateral Scribble:
   Two handed Marker drawing (1 Marker/crayon for each hand): Each movement is done for 9-10 seconds. We encourage the children to look at their marks on the paper, the teacher can stand at the front of the group and demonstrate on the chalkboard, describing the process of bilateral scribbling **(Younger children may need help with taping and movements at first):**
   1. Tape Paper onto table (horizontally).
   2. Make Random Marks with both hands.
   3. Make Vertical Lines beginning from the bottom of the paper to the top, up and down. (can alternate hands).
   4. Make Horizontal Lines, across paper with each hand on opposite edge of page," bringing their markers to meet in the middle. Have children cross the midline (cross arms to opposite sides of the paper and back to opposite side of page-repeat)
   5. Make two Arcs, or windshield wiper movements, back and forth. Let the Arcs move into two large circles and go around and around.
   6. Continue to make Circles in the reverse direction,- reverse again/repeating.

Start Up!   Facilitator Manual

ACTING IN A FEELING / ACTING OUT A FEELING

WEEK 5

A. Bi-Lateral Scribble Cont.:
7. Make gentle Dots- now go up and down on the paper, now back and forth across the paper.
8. Put one arm and hand over the other and make a Big X and now move the other arm and hand on top, now the other on top (repeat 4-5 times)
9. Make Fast Circles, go around really fast, now gradually slower and smaller, until you have a small circle add dot in the middle of the smallest circle, and STOP.

B. Bi-Lateral Drawing:
Flip paper and re-tape paper to table
With markers in each hand children are instructed to:
1. Draw Waterline
2. Draw Mountains
3. Draw birds
4. Draw fish in the river

MOTIVATION: "We all have feelings. Some of them are positive and some of them are negative. Today we are going to pick a feeling and describe it."

C. Acting In A Feeling / Acting Out A Feeling
1. Put paper on desk horizontally and draw a line down the middle of the paper.
2. Have the children think of a feeling. If younger children- choose a feeling for them: "sad" (when someone takes a toy from you), etc.
3. Label on left side of the paper "How Others See Me."
4. Label on the right side of the paper "How I See Myself."
5. Have children draw themselves how others see them when experiencing this feeling.
6. Have children draw how they see themselves when experiencing this feeling.
7. On the other side of the paper draw themselves acting out this feeling in the best possible way.
8. *Teacher:* **How do you think your grandparents and ancestors would want you to act when experiencing this feeling?**
10. Share with class.

CLOSURE/ DISCUSSION

- What was hard/ what was easy?
- What was your favorite part?
- What did you learn about yourself today?

Facilitator Manual — Start Up! — 71

WEEK 6

ANGER COLLAGE

PROBLEM PHASE

Purpose:
Emotional Homeostasis

Goal:
Exploration of Feelings and Perceptions

Neural Activity:
Limbic

Benefits:
- Identity Formation
- Emotional Regulation
- Emotional Expression
- Community Building
- Transforming Negative to Positive

Duration:
12 Weeks

Session 1 - Monday

ACTIVITY: ANGER COLLAGE

Art Materials:
- Markers
- 2 Pieces each of 9 x 12 paper
- Oil Pastels
- Glue
- A piece of large craft paper

SIMON SAYS

BREATHING / MEDITATION
"Close your eyes or leave them open if you really need to. Breathe in deeply through your nose or mouth, until your lungs are full. Let your breath out until your lungs are empty. Sit comfortably, feel feet on the ground. Imagine a safe place; a place where you feel good, a place where you feel peace."

ART DIRECTIVES:
A. Bi-Lateral Scribble:
   Two handed Marker drawing (1 Marker/crayon for each hand): Each movement is done for 9-10 seconds. We encourage the children to look at their marks on the paper, the teacher can stand at the front of the group and demonstrate on the chalkboard, describing the process of bilateral scribbling **(Younger children may need help with taping and movements at first):**
   1. Tape Paper onto table (horizontally).
   2. Make Random Marks with both hands.
   3. Make Vertical Lines beginning from the bottom of the paper to the top, up and down. (can alternate hands).
   4. Make Horizontal Lines, across paper with each hand on opposite edge of page," bringing their markers to meet in the middle. Have children cross the midline (cross arms to opposite sides of the paper and back to opposite side of page-repeat)
   5. Make two Arcs, or windshield wiper movements, back and forth. Let the Arcs move into two large circles and go around and around.
   6. Continue to make Circles in the reverse direction,- reverse again/ repeating.

ANGER COLLAGE

WEEK 6

A. Bi-Lateral Scribble Cont.:
7. Make gentle Dots- now go up and down on the paper, now back and forth across the paper.
8. Put one arm and hand over the other and make a Big X and now move the other arm and hand on top, now the other on top (repeat 4-5 times)
9. Make Fast Circles, go around really fast, now gradually slower and smaller, until you have a small circle add dot in the middle of the smallest circle, and STOP.

B. Bi-Lateral Drawing:
Flip paper and re-tape paper to table
With markers in each hand children are instructed to:
1. Draw a groundline
2. Draw a house from another culture with windows and door (tipi, wigwam, hut, traditional home, can add cultural teachings about traditional homes of particular population)
3. Draw a tree
4. Draw a basket of apples underneath the tree (or can be traditional food and add cultural teachings about the traditional foods of particular population)
5. Put clouds up in the sky
6. Sun / Birds

MOTIVATION: "Last time we explored our feelings and emotions. Today we are going to explore them a little more. Think about something that made you mad at some time in your life."

C. Anger Collage
1. Think about something that made you mad.
2. Let it out of your body.
3. Push hard on the oil pastels.
4. Rip the anger images into medium sized pieces.
5. Make a community collage by gluing the pieces of anger onto large craft paper, transforming the anger into a positive image.
6. *Teacher:* **Notice how we can transform something negative like anger, into something positive like this beautiful art piece.**
7. Take time to look at the collage as a class.

CLOSURE/ DISCUSSION

- What was it like to express that anger?

- How did it feel to get rid of it? To rip it up and transform it?

- What would happen if we didn't make a positive art piece out of our anger, if we let the anger stay?

- How is it healthier to do this than express it on each other?

- What was it like to do this?

Facilitator Manual Start Up!

WEEK 6

ANGER BOXES

PROBLEM PHASE

Purpose:
Emotional Homeostasis

Goal:
Exploration of Feelings and Perceptions

Neural Activity:
Limbic

Benefits:
- Emotional Expression
- Emotional Regulation
- Identity Formation

Duration:
12 Weeks

Session 2 - Friday

ACTIVITY: ANGER BOXES

Art Materials:
- Markers
- Pencils
- 1 Piece each of 9 x 12 paper
- 2" paper squares
- Sm. Boxes (can make from paper or old tea or toothpaste boxes)
- Tape
- Paint, Glitter, jewels, decorative objects

HEAD SHOULDERS KNEES & TOES

BREATHING / MEDITATION
"Close your eyes and breathe deeply. Imagine you are sitting next to a creek. You are feeling sad or worried about something in your life. Imagine you pick up a big green leaf. You begin to fold it into a box. Imagine you put your sadness and worry inside the leaf box and place it into the creek. The creek's current takes the leaf box down stream. You watch your little leaf box disappear until you can no longer see it. You worries and sadness are gone."

ART DIRECTIVES:
A. Bi-Lateral Scribble:
   Two handed Marker drawing (1 Marker/crayon for each hand): Each movement is done for 9-10 seconds. We encourage the children to look at their marks on the paper, the teacher can stand at the front of the group and demonstrate on the chalkboard, describing the process of bilateral scribbling **(Younger children may need help with taping and movements at first):**
  1. Tape Paper onto table (horizontally).
  2. Make Random Marks with both hands.
  3. Make Vertical Lines beginning from the bottom of the paper to the top, up and down. (can alternate hands).
  4. Make Horizontal Lines, across paper with each hand on opposite edge of page," bringing their markers to meet in the middle. Have children cross the midline (cross arms to opposite sides of the paper and back to opposite side of page-repeat)
  5. Make two Arcs, or windshield wiper movements, back and forth. Let the Arcs move into two large circles and go around and around.
  6. Continue to make Circles in the reverse direction,- reverse again/ repeating.

Start Up! Facilitator Manual

ANGER BOXES

WEEK 6

A. Bi-Lateral Scribble Cont.:
7. Make gentle Dots- now go up and down on the paper, now back and forth across the paper.
8. Put one arm and hand over the other and make a Big X and now move the other arm and hand on top, now the other on top (repeat 4-5 times)
9. Make Fast Circles, go around really fast, now gradually slower and smaller, until you have a small circle add dot in the middle of the smallest circle, and STOP.

B. Bi-Lateral Drawing:
Flip paper and re-tape paper to table
With markers in each hand children are instructed to:
1. Draw a starry sky
2. Draw some star people (can add cultural teachings about traditional star knowledge beliefs of particular population)
3. Draw a spaceship
4. Draw a moon

MOTIVATION: "Last time we made a beautiful collage from the art that we made from releasing our anger that we had from a time in our lives. Today we are going to think of something we are angry about currently."

C. Anger Boxes
1. On 2" paper squares- write down things or symbols that represent what you are currently angry about.
2. Enclose paper squares in the box and tape the box closed.
3. Decorate the boxes with wood, jewels, paint, glitter, etc.
4. *Teacher:* **We have the ability to transform our negative feelings and experiences into something positive- just like we did with our anger collage. You can't undo it, but can transform it into something positive.**
5. Share with class.

CLOSURE/ DISCUSSION

- How can you change something you don't like about yourself?

- Is there something in your box you would feel comfortable sharing?

- What did you notice or learn about yourself today?

Facilitator Manual — Start Up!

WEEK 7

WHEN I AM STRESSED / NOT STRESSED

PROBLEM PHASE

Purpose:
Emotional Homeostasis

Goal:
Exploration of Feelings and Perceptions

Neural Activity:
Limbic

Benefits:
- Emotional Identification
- Emotional Expression
- Identity Formation
- Emotional Regulation
- Adaptive Coping Skills

Duration:
12 Weeks

Session 1 - Monday

ACTIVITY: WHEN I AM STRESSED / NOT STRESSED

Art Materials:
- Markers
- 2 Pieces each of 9 x 12 paper
- Oil Pastels

MUSIC FREEZE

BREATHING / MEDITATION
"Close your eyes or leave them open if you really need to. Breathe in deeply through your nose or mouth, until your lungs are full. Let your breath out until your lungs are empty. Sit comfortably, feel feet on the ground. Breathe in and imagine a white light filling your body. Let it out. Imagine a color that represents your stress. Where in your body is this stress color? Breathe in the white light and let it take over your stress. Breathe out the stress color. Breathe in white light into your entire body, from your toes to the top of your head."

ART DIRECTIVES:
A. Bi-Lateral Scribble:
   Two handed Marker drawing (1 Marker/crayon for each hand): Each movement is done for 9-10 seconds. We encourage the children to look at their marks on the paper, the teacher can stand at the front of the group and demonstrate on the chalkboard, describing the process of bilateral scribbling **(Younger children may need help with taping and movements at first):**
   1. Tape Paper onto table (horizontally).
   2. Make Random Marks with both hands.
   3. Make Vertical Lines beginning from the bottom of the paper to the top, up and down. (can alternate hands).
   4. Make Horizontal Lines, across paper with each hand on opposite edge of page," bringing their markers to meet in the middle. Have children cross the midline (cross arms to opposite sides of the paper and back to opposite side of page-repeat)
   5. Make two Arcs, or windshield wiper movements, back and forth. Let the Arcs move into two large circles and go around and around.
   6. Continue to make Circles in the reverse direction,- reverse again/ repeating.

76   Start Up!   Facilitator Manual

WHEN I AM STRESSED / NOT STRESSED

WEEK 7

A. Bi-Lateral Scribble Cont.:
7. Make gentle Dots- now go up and down on the paper, now back and forth across the paper.
8. Put one arm and hand over the other and make a Big X and now move the other arm and hand on top, now the other on top (repeat 4-5 times)
9. Make Fast Circles, go around really fast, now gradually slower and smaller, until you have a small circle add dot in the middle of the smallest circle, and STOP.

B. Bi-Lateral Drawing:
Flip paper and re-tape paper to table
With markers in each hand children are instructed to:
1. Draw a waterline
2. Draw a boat (can be a traditional boat of particular population and add cultural teachings)
3. Draw a motor or sails to the boat (if applicable)
4. Draw a flag
5. Draw someone fishing with a line in the water with a hook
6. Draw some fish in the water
7. Add a shark
8. Draw a starfish in the water
9. Add clouds/sun/birds

MOTIVATION: "We all experience stress in life. What is stress? There is good stress, like when your team is playing or you are going to talk in front of a crowd; this kind of stress helps us to do well. There is also stress that is not good for us, like when we worry about something. Today we are going to explore how we feel when we are stressed."

C. When I Am Stressed / Not Stressed
1. Put paper horizontal on desk and draw a line down the middle of the page. Label left section "When I am stressed I_____."
2. Have children draw shapes and symbols representing their stress.
3. Label the right section " When I am not stressed, I_____."
4. Have the children draw symbols and shapes representing when they are not stressed.
5. **Teacher: "It is important to notice where the stress is in your body so you can breathe deeply and let it go."**

CLOSURE/ DISCUSSION

- Where do you notice the stress in your body?

- What do you notice when you aren't stressed?

- Who is your support system?

- What did you learn about yourself?

Facilitator Manual — Start Up!

WEEK 7

PARTNER SCULPTURE

PROBLEM PHASE

Purpose:
Emotional Homeostasis

Goal:
Exploration of Feelings and Perceptions

Neural Activity:
Limbic

Benefits:
- Community Building
- Expressing Wants/ Needs
- Self Expression
- Identity Formation

Duration:
12 Weeks

Session 2 - Friday

ACTIVITY: PARTNER SCULPTURE

Art Materials:
- Markers
- 1 Piece each of 9 x 12 paper
- Cereal Boxes
- Toothpaste/ tea boxes,
- Coffee cans
- Masking tape
- Fabric
- Yarn
- Paint in cups
- Brushes

SIMON SAYS

BREATHING / MEDITATION
"Close your eyes and breathe deeply. Imagine your ancestors and how they lived a long time ago. They may have had tools that helped them make their lives a little easier; like the bow and arrow, spear, tools from animal bones and stone, tools to help plant and grow food, and tools to build homes. Imagine one of your ancestors comes to you and tells you to build something important. Imagine what your ancestor instructs you to make and imagine making it."

ART DIRECTIVES:

A. Bi-Lateral Scribble:
  Two handed Marker drawing (1 Marker/crayon for each hand): Each movement is done for 9-10 seconds. We encourage the children to look at their marks on the paper, the teacher can stand at the front of the group and demonstrate on the chalkboard, describing the process of bilateral scribbling **(Younger children may need help with taping and movements at first):**
  1. Tape Paper onto table (horizontally).
  2. Make Random Marks with both hands.
  3. Make Vertical Lines beginning from the bottom of the paper to the top, up and down. (can alternate hands).
  4. Make Horizontal Lines, across paper with each hand on opposite edge of page," bringing their markers to meet in the middle. Have children cross the midline (cross arms to opposite sides of the paper and back to opposite side of page-repeat)
  5. Make two Arcs, or windshield wiper movements, back and forth. Let the Arcs move into two large circles and go around and around.

PARTNER SCULPTURE

WEEK 7

A. Bi-Lateral Scribble Cont.:
7. Make gentle Dots- now go up and down on the paper, now back and forth across the paper.
8. Put one arm and hand over the other and make a Big X and now move the other arm and hand on top, now the other on top (repeat 4-5 times)
9. Make Fast Circles, go around really fast, now gradually slower and smaller, until you have a small circle add dot in the middle of the smallest circle, and STOP.

B. Bi-Lateral Drawing:
Flip paper and re-tape paper to table
With markers in each hand children are instructed to:
1. Draw a groundline
2. Draw a dinosaur (or animal special to traditions of particular population, buffalo, whale, jaguar, etc. Include cultural teachings of animal)
3. Draw tree
4. Draw a sun
5. Draw another animal

MOTIVATION: "Inventing is fun. There are so many inventions in the world ; have the class name a couple inventions. Today we are going to create our own inventions: invent a machine that is a new method of transportation, or something that you think kids need."

C. Partner Sculpture
1. Have the children pair up with a partner.
2. Think of an idea together of a new invention: a new method of transportation or something you think kids need.
3. Build your invention using cereal/ toothpaste/ tea boxes, coffee cans, masking tape, paint, fabric.
4. Have children share if they wish.

CLOSURE/ DISCUSSION

- What was it like to work together ?

- Are you more of a leader of follower?

- What feelings came up in your role?

- If you wanted to give up because things weren't going your way, that might mean you might like to work alone at a job, others might prefer to work in groups. It might be good to know this about yourself.

Facilitator Manual Start Up!

WEEK 8

PRAYER FLAGS

PROBLEM PHASE

Purpose:
Emotional Homeostasis

Goal:
Exploration of Feelings and Perceptions

Neural Activity:
Limbic

Benefits:
• Identify support
• Define/describe loss
• Emotional Regulation

Duration:
12 Weeks

Session 1 - Monday

ACTIVITY: PRAYER FLAGS (to memorialize death of loved one/community member)

Art Materials:
• Markers
• 2 Pieces of 9 x 12 paper
• Masking Tape
• Paint in cups
• Brushes
• String

HEAD SHOULDERS KNEES & TOES

BREATHING / MEDITATION
"Close your eyes and breathe deeply. Think about a person you once knew of or knew personally, who is no longer living. Think about the positive things they did, which somehow positively affected you. Think about what it is you learned from this person. Imagine a symbol or a shape, which represents them and your gratitude for what they taught you."

ART DIRECTIVES:
A. Bi-Lateral Scribble:
   Two handed Marker drawing (1 Marker/crayon for each hand): Each movement is done for 9-10 seconds. We encourage the children to look at their marks on the paper, the teacher can stand at the front of the group and demonstrate on the chalkboard, describing the process of bilateral scribbling **(Younger children may need help with taping and movements at first):**
  1. Tape Paper onto table (horizontally).
  2. Make Random Marks with both hands.
  3. Make Vertical Lines beginning from the bottom of the paper to the top, up and down. (can alternate hands).
  4. Make Horizontal Lines, across paper with each hand on opposite edge of page," bringing their markers to meet in the middle. Have children cross the midline (cross arms to opposite sides of the paper and back to opposite side of page-repeat)
  5. Make two Arcs, or windshield wiper movements, back and forth. Let the Arcs move into two large circles and go around and around.
  6. Continue to make Circles in the reverse direction,- reverse again/ repeating.

PRAYER FLAGS

WEEK 8

A. Bi-Lateral Scribble Cont.:
7. Make gentle Dots- now go up and down on the paper, now back and forth across the paper.
8. Put one arm and hand over the other and make a Big X and now move the other arm and hand on top, now the other on top (repeat 4-5 times)
9. Make Fast Circles, go around really fast, now gradually slower and smaller, until you have a small circle add dot in the middle of the smallest circle, and STOP.

B. Bi-Lateral Drawing:
Flip paper and re-tape paper to table
With markers in each hand children are instructed to:
1. Draw a groundline
2. Draw some flowers
3. Draw some ladybugs
4. Draw some spiders
5. Draw some mosquitoes

MOTIVATION: Normalizes social taboos such as crying. "When we lose someone we feel a lot of feelings; sadness, anger, confusion. This is normal to feel these feelings at a time like this. When we think about the loss of someone, tears help us to manage our emotions, by helping us to release our sadness. Onions make us cry just like sadness makes us cry. It's ok to cry and it is ok to cry in front of others. You might think of all the losses you have ever had. This is how we learn to cope through loss."

C. Prayer Flags
1. Have children fold over the top inch of their paper vertically to make a flag.
2. Draw or paint figures, symbols and shapes to represent feelings of loss of loved one or community member.
3. Play soft music.
4. When images are complete have the children string the flags together and hang from wall to wall across the classroom.
5. **Teacher: You can sing a memorial song, or add any culturally appropriate ritual to acknowledge loved one's and the feelings of the students. The students can give flags to family of deceased.**
6. Students can share if they choose.

CLOSURE/ DISCUSSION

- Say one word to describe how you feel right now.

Facilitator Manual Start Up! 81

WEEK 8

WHEN I AM ANXIOUS / WHEN I AM NOT ANXIOUS

PROBLEM PHASE

Purpose:
Emotional Homeostasis

Goal:
Exploration of Feelings and Perceptions

Neural Activity:
Limbic

Benefits:
- Expressing Emotions
- Emotional Containment
- Self Awareness
- Emotional Regulation•

Duration:
12 Weeks

Session 2 - Friday

ACTIVITY: WHEN I AM ANXIOUS / WHEN I AM NOT ANXIOUS

Art Materials:
- Markers
- 2 pieces of 9 x 12 paper

MUSIC FREEZE

BREATHING / MEDITATION
"Close your eyes and breathe deeply. Feel your body with the weight of gravity. Imagine anything that is currently making you feel nervous or anxious. It might be a big exam coming up, it might be a personal problem. Imagine you are walking through the mountains. You see some smoke in the distance, but it is not smoke, it is steam from a nearby hotspring. The water is bubbling up from the ground into a beautiful pool. Imagine yourself getting into the warm water and melting your anxiety away. Feel the water healing you and taking out all your nervousness.

ART DIRECTIVES:
A. Bi-Lateral Scribble:
   Two handed Marker drawing (1 Marker/crayon for each hand): Each movement is done for 9-10 seconds. We encourage the children to look at their marks on the paper, the teacher can stand at the front of the group and demonstrate on the chalkboard, describing the process of bilateral scribbling **(Younger children may need help with taping and movements at first):**
  1. Tape Paper onto table (horizontally).
  2. Make Random Marks with both hands.
  3. Make Vertical Lines beginning from the bottom of the paper to the top, up and down. (can alternate hands).
  4. Make Horizontal Lines, across paper with each hand on opposite edge of page," bringing their markers to meet in the middle. Have children cross the midline (cross arms to opposite sides of the paper and back to opposite side of page-repeat)
  5. Make two Arcs, or windshield wiper movements, back and forth. Let the Arcs move into two large circles and go around and around.
  6. Continue to make Circles in the reverse direction,- reverse again/ repeating.

Start Up!   Facilitator Manual

WHEN I AM ANXIOUS / WHEN I AM NOT ANXIOUS

WEEK 8

A. Bi-Lateral Scribble Cont.:
7. Make gentle Dots- now go up and down on the paper, now back and forth across the paper.
8. Put one arm and hand over the other and make a Big X and now move the other arm and hand on top, now the other on top (repeat 4-5 times)
9. Make Fast Circles, go around really fast, now gradually slower and smaller, until you have a small circle add dot in the middle of the smallest circle, and STOP.

B. Bi-Lateral Drawing:
Flip paper and re-tape paper to table
With markers in each hand children are instructed to:
1. Draw a groundline
2. Draw a cactus
3. Draw a desert
4. Draw a skull
5. Draw another cactus
6. Draw a coyote
7. Draw a moon

MOTIVATION: "Who knows what anxiety is? Anxiety feels like a shakiness inside and can feel like nervousness. It might be because we are worried about something, or scared about something. Everyone has felt anxious at times. Who here has felt anxious before, raise your hand? Today we are going to do some art about feeling anxious."

C. When I am Anxious / When I am Not Anxious
1. Put paper horizontal on desk and draw a line down the middle of the page.
2. Label left section "When I am anxious, I_____."
3. Have children draw shapes and symbols representing their anxiety.
4. Label the right section " When I am not anxious, I_____."
5. Have the children draw symbols and shapes representing when they are not anxious.
6. *Teacher:* **Where do you notice the anxiety in your body? What do you notice when you aren't anxious?**
   It is important to notice where the stress is in your body so you can breathe deeply and let it go. You can burn sage, copal, etc to purify feelings.

CLOSURE/ DISCUSSION

- Who is your support system?

- What did you learn about yourself?

Facilitator Manual — Start Up!

WEEK 9

COPING WHEEL

PROBLEM PHASE

Purpose:
Emotional Homeostasis

Goal:
Exploration of Feelings and Perceptions

Neural Activity:
Limbic

Benefits:
- Emotional Recognition
- Emotional Expression
- Learning Adaptive Coping Strategies
- Prevention

Duration:
12 Weeks

Session 1 - Monday

ACTIVITY: COPING WHEEL

Art Materials:
- Markers
- 1 Piece each of 9 x 12 paper
- Round Piece of Paper
- Magazines
- Glue Sticks
- Scissors

SIMON SAYS

BREATHING / MEDITATION
"Close your eyes and breathe deeply. Think back to the meditation when you were in full control of the way you acted during a difficult emotion. Imagine you are feeling another difficult emotion and imagine the healthiest way you could cope with it. Imagine working through the difficult emotion. Imagine how you feel about being in control of yourself. Imagine this new, healthier way of coping becomes the way you respond every time you feel this emotion."

ART DIRECTIVES:
A. Bi-Lateral Scribble:
   Two handed Marker drawing (1 Marker/crayon for each hand): Each movement is done for 9-10 seconds. We encourage the children to look at their marks on the paper, the teacher can stand at the front of the group and demonstrate on the chalkboard, describing the process of bilateral scribbling **(Younger children may need help with taping and movements at first):**
   1. Tape Paper onto table (horizontally).
   2. Make Random Marks with both hands.
   3. Make Vertical Lines beginning from the bottom of the paper to the top, up and down. (can alternate hands).
   4. Make Horizontal Lines, across paper with each hand on opposite edge of page," bringing their markers to meet in the middle. Have children cross the midline (cross arms to opposite sides of the paper and back to opposite side of page-repeat)
   5. Make two Arcs, or windshield wiper movements, back and forth. Let the Arcs move into two large circles and go around and around.
   6. Continue to make Circles in the reverse direction,- reverse again/ repeating.

Start Up!   Facilitator Manual

COPING WHEEL

WEEK 9

A. Bi-Lateral Scribble Cont.:
7. Make gentle Dots- now go up and down on the paper, now back and forth across the paper.
8. Put one arm and hand over the other and make a Big X and now move the other arm and hand on top, now the other on top (repeat 4-5 times)
9. Make Fast Circles, go around really fast, now gradually slower and smaller, until you have a small circle add dot in the middle of the smallest circle, and STOP.

B. Bi-Lateral Drawing:
Flip paper and re-tape paper to table
With markers in each hand children are instructed to:
1. Draw Waterline
2. Draw Mountains
3. Draw birds
4. Draw fish in the river

MOTIVATION: "Can anyone tell me what coping means? Coping means the positive ways that we deal with difficult feelings. If you feel stressed, what are some positive ways to cope with that feeling? You might go for a walk, or deep breathe, meditate, take a bath, spend time with friends, do art, etc. Today we are going to make coping wheels, that will help us identify how we cope certain emotions."

C. Coping Wheel
1. Have the children draw a line vertically and horizontally on the circle shaped paper to make a "pie" with 4 sections.
2. Ask children to cut out 4 pictures from magazines which represent coping skills that they use in their lives, and glue 1 into each of the 4 sections. (If they cannot find the right magazine pictures, invite them to draw it in the section).

CLOSURE/ DISCUSSION

- Which one works best?

- Which one do you use most often?

- Keep this on your wall in your bedroom and use it when you are feeling difficult feelings.

Facilitator Manual — Start Up!

WEEK 9

KINDNESS TOWARD OTHERS

PROBLEM PHASE

Purpose:
Emotional Homeostasis

Goal:
Exploration of Feelings and Perceptions

Neural Activity:
Limbic

Benefits:
- Community building
- Social skills
- Reinforcing positive emotions

Duration:
12 Weeks

Session 2 - Friday

ACTIVITY: KINDNESS TOWARDS OTHERS

Art Materials:
- Markers
- 2 Pieces each of 9 x 12 paper
- Oil Pastels
- Chalk Pastels

HEAD SHOULDERS KNEES & TOES

BREATHING / MEDITATION

"Close your eyes and breathe deeply. Imagine someone doing something very kind for you. This kindness makes you feel warm inside and very good. Imagine you know someone who is in need of some kindness. Imagine you do something kind for them. What might it be? Imagine how this person might feel and act toward you afterward. Imagine how this act of kindness makes you feel? Take 3 deep breaths and gently open your eyes."

ART DIRECTIVES:

A. Bi-Lateral Scribble:

Two handed Marker drawing (1 Marker/crayon for each hand): Each movement is done for 9-10 seconds. We encourage the children to look at their marks on the paper, the teacher can stand at the front of the group and demonstrate on the chalkboard, describing the process of bilateral scribbling **(Younger children may need help with taping and movements at first):**

1. Tape Paper onto table (horizontally).
2. Make Random Marks with both hands.
3. Make Vertical Lines beginning from the bottom of the paper to the top, up and down. (can alternate hands).
4. Make Horizontal Lines, across paper with each hand on opposite edge of page," bringing their markers to meet in the middle. Have children cross the midline (cross arms to opposite sides of the paper and back to opposite side of page-repeat)
5. Make two Arcs, or windshield wiper movements, back and forth. Let the Arcs move into two large circles and go around and around.

Start Up!

KINDNESS TOWARD OTHERS

WEEK 9

A. Bi-Lateral Scribble Cont.:
6. Continue to make Circles in the reverse direction,- reverse again/ repeating.
7. Make gentle Dots- now go up and down on the paper, now back and forth across the paper.
8. Put one arm and hand over the other and make a Big X and now move the other arm and hand on top, now the other on top (repeat 4-5 times)
9. Make Fast Circles, go around really fast, now gradually slower and smaller, until you have a small circle add dot in the middle of the smallest circle, and STOP.

B. Bi-Lateral Drawing:
Flip paper and re-tape paper to table
With markers in each hand children are instructed to:
1. Draw a sky
2. Draw a moon
3. Draw stars
4. Draw planets
5. Draw a spaceship
6. Draw a star being (alien)

MOTIVATION: "Who likes it when others are kind to us? Who likes to be kind to others? Today we are going to draw a picture of a time when we were kind to someone."

C. Kindness Towards Others
1. Have children draw with markers and pastels a time when they were kind to someone.
2. Share with class (this helps peers to learn more ways to be kind).

CLOSURE/ DISCUSSION

- How did you feel when you were kind to someone?

- What was the person's response?

Facilitator Manual — Start Up!

WEEK 10

ROCKET SHIP

PROBLEM PHASE

Purpose:
Emotional Homeostasis

Goal:
Exploration of Feelings and Perceptions

Neural Activity:
Limbic

Benefits:
• Addressing Loss
• Identity Formation
• Identifying Priorities

Duration:
12 Weeks

Session 1 - Monday

ACTIVITY: ROCKET SHIP

Art Materials:
• Markers
• 2 Pieces each of 9 x 12 paper
• Construction Paper
• Glue Sticks
• Scissors

MUSIC FREEZE

BREATHING / MEDITATION
"Close your eyes and breathe deeply. Imagine you are walking through a forest. Imagine you are carrying a basket of the 5 most important things to you in your life. It is a very bumpy path and one by one your important things fall out of the basket. Imagine you reach the end of the path and look down into your basket to realize all of your important things are gone except the most important one. What is left in the basket? Imagine you turn around and go back down the path to collect you're the things that feel out of your basket. One by one, you find your important things. Feel what it's like to have found these things again. Take 3 deep breaths and gently open your eyes."

ART DIRECTIVES:
 A. Bi-Lateral Scribble:
   Two handed Marker drawing (1 Marker/crayon for each hand): Each movement is done for 9-10 seconds. We encourage the children to look at their marks on the paper, the teacher can stand at the front of the group and demonstrate on the chalkboard, describing the process of bilateral scribbling **(Younger children may need help with taping and movements at first):**
  1. Tape Paper onto table (horizontally).
  2. Make Random Marks with both hands.
  3. Make Vertical Lines beginning from the bottom of the paper to the top, up and down. (can alternate hands).
  4. Make Horizontal Lines, across paper with each hand on opposite edge of page," bringing their markers to meet in the middle. Have children cross the midline (cross arms to opposite sides of the paper and back to opposite side of page-repeat)
  5. Make two Arcs, or windshield wiper movements, back and forth. Let the Arcs move into two large circles and go around and around.
  6. Continue to make Circles in the reverse direction,- reverse again/ repeating.
  7. Make gentle Dots- now go up and down on the paper, now back and forth across the paper.

ROCKET SHIP

WEEK 10

A. Bi-Lateral Scribble Cont.:
8. Put one arm and hand over the other and make a Big X and now move the other arm and hand on top, now the other on top (repeat 4-5 times)
9. Make Fast Circles, go around really fast, now gradually slower and smaller, until you have a small circle add dot in the middle of the smallest circle, and STOP.

B. Bi-Lateral Drawing:
Flip paper and re-tape paper to table
With markers in each hand children are instructed to:
1. Draw a starry sky
2. Draw some star people (can add cultural teachings about traditional star knowledge beliefs of particular population)
3. Draw a spaceship
4. Draw a moon

C. Scribble Chase
1. Select a partner (each child has 1 marker)
2. Determine who will be the leader, the follower
3. Say "GO" and the leader leads with the marker and the follower tries to follow the leader on the paper with their marker (30-40 seconds each turn)
4. Switch roles

MOTIVATION: "Who has gone on a trip or a vacation and had to remember all the things you would need while away from home? Today we are going to make rocketships and we need to pack all the things that are important to us."

D. Rocket Ship
1. Each child folds a piece of paper in half lengthwise and cuts off the tip to make a rocket ship shape.
2. **Teacher:** "We will be leaving on our rocket ships. You will be safe and you will come back very soon. What would be the things you would bring?"
3. Have children cut out symbols from construction paper to represent things of importance and stick them onto their rocket ships.
4. **Teacher:** "I just got a call from the ship…Oh, you have to give up one thing, what thing will you give up? Take it off the ship and keep it on your desk." **Note: If Giving up objects generated anxiety, don't force the child to give it up.**
5. Repeat the above step of removing objects until only one is left on the rocket ship.
6. **Teacher:** "I just got another call from the ship… you can now put everything back on the ship
7. Have children glue symbols onto ship.

CLOSURE/DISCUSSION

- What did you learn about what matters to you?

- What was the thing you couldn't do without first?

Facilitator Manual Start Up! 89

WEEK 10

FRIENDSHIP

PROBLEM PHASE

Purpose:
Emotional Homeostasis

Goal:
Exploration of Feelings and Perceptions

Neural Activity:
Limbic

Benefits:
- Identity Formation
- Developing Priorities
- Social Skills

Duration:
12 Weeks

Session 2 - Friday

ACTIVITY: FRIENDSHIP

Art Materials:
- Markers
- 3 Pieces each of 9 x 12 paper
- Oil Pastels

SIMON SAYS

BREATHING / MEDITATION
"Close your eyes and breathe deeply. Imagine you are with your closest friend. Imagine you are sitting under a tree together in the shade during a hot summer day. Imagine feeling very safe with your friend, like you can trust them to tell them anything. Imagine your friend holds out their hand and puts something in your hand. You open your hand and you see something very special, which will remind you of your friend's love and support always. Imagine what that feels like to feel this love. Take 3 deep breaths and gently open your eyes."

ART DIRECTIVES:

A. **Bi-Lateral Scribble:**
   Two handed Marker drawing (1 Marker/crayon for each hand): Each movement is done for 9-10 seconds. We encourage the children to look at their marks on the paper, the teacher can stand at the front of the group and demonstrate on the chalkboard, describing the process of bilateral scribbling **(Younger children may need help with taping and movements at first):**
   1. Tape Paper onto table (horizontally).
   2. Make Random Marks with both hands.
   3. Make Vertical Lines beginning from the bottom of the paper to the top, up and down. (can alternate hands).
   4. Make Horizontal Lines, across paper with each hand on opposite edge of page," bringing their markers to meet in the middle. Have children cross the midline (cross arms to opposite sides of the paper and back to opposite side of page-repeat)
   5. Make two Arcs, or windshield wiper movements, back and forth. Let the Arcs move into two large circles and go around and around.

Start Up! — Facilitator Manual

FRIENDSHIP

WEEK 10

A. Bi-Lateral Scribble Cont.:
6. Continue to make Circles in the reverse direction,- reverse again/ repeating.
7. Make gentle Dots- now go up and down on the paper, now back and forth across the paper.
8. Put one arm and hand over the other and make a Big X and now move the other arm and hand on top, now the other on top (repeat 4-5 times)
9. Make Fast Circles, go around really fast, now gradually slower and smaller, until you have a small circle add dot in the middle of the smallest circle, and STOP.

B. Bi-Lateral Drawing:
Flip paper and re-tape paper to table
With markers in each hand children are instructed to:
1. Draw a groundline
2. Draw favorite animal
3. Draw tree
4. Draw a sun
5. Draw another animal of same type

MOTIVATION: "What qualities do you want in a friendship? Who thinks honesty is important in a friendship, raise your hand? Who thinks being a good listener is important? Today we are going to draw what qualities you want in your friendships."

C. Friendship
1. With oil pastels have children draw on one side of the paper the qualities they want in their friendships.
2. On the other side of the paper have the children draw: "What quality of being a good friend can you work on this week?"
3. Share with class- If someone shares "honesty" ask class to raise their hands if they also chose that quality. Repeat with each new quality a child shares.

CLOSURE/ DISCUSSION

- Was this easy or hard?

- What did you like most?

- What did you like least?

Start Up!

WEEK 11

GIVING TO THE WORLD

PROBLEM PHASE

Purpose:
Emotional Homeostasis

Goal:
Exploration of Feelings and Perceptions

Neural Activity:
Limbic

Benefits:
• Identity formation
• Developing Altruism
• Installation of Hope
• Community Building

Duration:
12 Weeks

Session 1 - Monday

ACTIVITY: GIVING TO THE WORLD

Art Materials:
• Markers
• 2 Pieces each of 9 x 12 paper
• Oil Pastels
• Chalk Pastels

HEAD SHOULDERS KNEES & TOES

BREATHING / MEDITATION
"Close your eyes and breathe deeply. Feel your feet on the floor. Imagine you are growing roots from the bottom of your feet into the floor. These roots grow down through the floor, into the ground, through the layers of rock and soil, deeply into the earth. Different cultures have different names for the earth. Many cultures refer to her as Mother Earth in their language, as she brings life to all of us. She grows us food. She gives us water, she grows everything we use to build houses and to live. What is the name for Mother Earth in your culture? Imagine any stress you may have leaving your body; down through these roots and into Mother Earth. Mother Earth is happy to help you by taking away your stress. Imagine feeling grateful to Mother Earth for her help. Imagine sending your gratitude for her down through your roots, into Mother Earth. Take 3 deep breaths and gently open your eyes."

ART DIRECTIVES:
  A. Bi-Lateral Scribble:
   Two handed Marker drawing (1 Marker/crayon for each hand): Each movement is done for 9-10 seconds. We encourage the children to look at their marks on the paper, the teacher can stand at the front of the group and demonstrate on the chalkboard, describing the process of bilateral scribbling **(Younger children may need help with taping and movements at first):**
  1. Tape Paper onto table (horizontally).
  2. Make Random Marks with both hands.
  3. Make Vertical Lines beginning from the bottom of the paper to the top, up and down. (can alternate hands).
  4. Make Horizontal Lines, across paper with each hand on opposite edge of page," bringing their markers to meet in the middle. Have children cross the midline (cross arms to opposite sides of the paper and back to opposite side of page-repeat)
  5. Make two Arcs, or windshield wiper movements, back and forth. Let the Arcs move into two large circles and go around and around.

Start Up!

GIVING TO THE WORLD

WEEK 11

A. Bi-Lateral Scribble Cont.:
6. Continue to make Circles in the reverse direction,- reverse again/ repeating.
7. Make gentle Dots- now go up and down on the paper, now back and forth across the paper.
8. Put one arm and hand over the other and make a Big X and now move the other arm and hand on top, now the other on top (repeat 4-5 times)
9. Make Fast Circles, go around really fast, now gradually slower and smaller, until you have a small circle add dot in the middle of the smallest circle, and STOP.

B. Bi-Lateral Drawing:
Flip paper and re-tape paper to table
With markers in each hand children are instructed to:
1. Draw a groundline
2. Draw some flowers
3. Draw some worms
4. Draw some spiders
5. Draw some mosquitoes

MOTIVATION: "If you were to give something to the world what would you give? It could be an object or an act of kindness, or anything you think of that could positively impact our world."

C. Giving To The World
1. "Imagine having impact on the world."
2. Have children draw an image of what they would give to the world.
3. Share images and have children tape images to the wall very close together to form a big patchwork quilt of images.
4. **Teacher: Emphasize that each child has the ability to do something good for the world, that we are all puzzle pieces within a big puzzle and we fit together. Emphasize that everyone belongs and everyone has something to offer to create a better world.**

CLOSURE/ DISCUSSION

- How would you feel giving?
- How would people feel receiving it?

Facilitator Manual — Start Up!

WEEK 11

COLLAGE OF FEELINGS

PROBLEM PHASE

Purpose:
Emotional Homeostasis

Goal:
Exploration of Feelings and Perceptions

Neural Activity:
Limbic

Benefits:
- Emotional Development
- Emotional Expression
- Emotional Regulation
- Identity Formation

Duration:
12 Weeks

Session 2 - Friday

ACTIVITY: COLLAGE OF FEELINGS

Art Materials:
- Markers
- 2 Pieces each of 9 x 12 paper
- Colored Tissue Paper
- School glue in small cups
- Sponge Brushes
- Scissors

MUSIC FREEZE

BREATHING / MEDITATION

"Close your eyes or leave them open if you really need to. Breathe in deeply through your nose or mouth, until your lungs are full. Let your breath out until your lungs are empty. Sit comfortably, feel feet on the ground. Breathe in and imagine a white light filling your body. Let it out. Imagine a color that represents your stress. Where in your body is this stress color? Breathe in the white light and let it take over your stress. Breathe out the stress color. Breathe in white light into your entire body, from your toes to the top of your head." Can set a timer for longer and longer times, up to 3-5 minutes.

ART DIRECTIVES:

A. Bi-Lateral Scribble:

Two handed Marker drawing (1 Marker/crayon for each hand): Each movement is done for 9-10 seconds. We encourage the children to look at their marks on the paper, the teacher can stand at the front of the group and demonstrate on the chalkboard, describing the process of bilateral scribbling **(Younger children may need help with taping and movements at first):**

1. Tape Paper onto table (horizontally).
2. Make Random Marks with both hands.
3. Make Vertical Lines beginning from the bottom of the paper to the top, up and down. (can alternate hands).
4. Make Horizontal Lines, across paper with each hand on opposite edge of page," bringing their markers to meet in the middle. Have children cross the midline (cross arms to opposite sides of the paper and back to opposite side of page-repeat)
5. Make two Arcs, or windshield wiper movements, back and forth. Let the Arcs move into two large circles and go around and around.

Start Up!   Facilitator Manual

COLLAGE OF FEELINGS

WEEK 11

A. Bi-Lateral Scribble Cont.:
6. Continue to make Circles in the reverse direction,- reverse again/repeating.
7. Make gentle Dots- now go up and down on the paper, now back and forth across the paper.
8. Put one arm and hand over the other and make a Big X and now move the other arm and hand on top, now the other on top (repeat 4-5 times)
9. Make Fast Circles, go around really fast, now gradually slower and smaller, until you have a small circle add dot in the middle of the smallest circle, and STOP.

B. Bi-Lateral Drawing:
Flip paper and re-tape paper to table
With markers in each hand children are instructed to:
1. Draw a groundline
2. Draw a cactus
3. Draw a desert
4. Draw a skull
5. Draw another cactus
6. Draw a coyote
7. Draw a moon

MOTIVATION: "We all experience different feelings. Some feelings are good, and some feelings are challenging. Today we are going to make a tissue paper collage of feelings".

C. Collage of Feelings
1. Cut out or tear shapes and symbols using tissue paper that represents: happy, sad, frustrated, confused, joyful, and scared.
2. Glue tissue paper symbols onto a big piece of paper.
3. You can lay the symbols anywhere on the page, and they can overlap.
4. Coat final image with glue and let dry.

CLOSURE/DISCUSSION

- Which feeling is there the most? The biggest?

- Which one is there the least? The smallest?

- Which one are you most comfortable with?

- Which one are you least comfortable with?

Facilitator Manual — Start Up!

WEEK 12

SOLVE A PROBLEM

PROBLEM PHASE

Purpose:
Emotional Homeostasis

Goal:
Exploration of Feelings and Perceptions

Neural Activity:
Limbic

Benefits:
- Fostering Problem Solving Skills
- Abstract Thinking
- Creating a Narrative
- Fostering Imagination
- Promotes Critical Thinking

Duration:
12 Weeks

Session 1 - Monday

ACTIVITY: SOLVE A PROBLEM

Art Materials:
- Markers
- 2 Pieces each of 9 x 12 paper
- Colored pencils

SIMON SAYS

BREATHING / MEDITATION
"Close your eyes or leave them open if you really need to. Breathe in deeply through your nose or mouth, until your lungs are full. Let your breath out until your lungs are empty. Sit comfortably, feel feet on the ground. Imagine a safe place; a place where you feel good, a place where you feel peace."

ART DIRECTIVES:

A. Bi-Lateral Scribble:

Two handed Marker drawing (1 Marker/crayon for each hand): Each movement is done for 9-10 seconds. We encourage the children to look at their marks on the paper, the teacher can stand at the front of the group and demonstrate on the chalkboard, describing the process of bilateral scribbling **(Younger children may need help with taping and movements at first):**

1. Tape Paper onto table (horizontally).
2. Make Random Marks with both hands.
3. Make Vertical Lines beginning from the bottom of the paper to the top, up and down. (can alternate hands).
4. Make Horizontal Lines, across paper with each hand on opposite edge of page," bringing their markers to meet in the middle. Have children cross the midline (cross arms to opposite sides of the paper and back to opposite side of page-repeat)
5. Make two Arcs, or windshield wiper movements, back and forth. Let the Arcs move into two large circles and go around and around.
6. Continue to make Circles in the reverse direction,- reverse again/ repeating.

SOLVE A PROBLEM

WEEK 12

A. Bi-Lateral Scribble Cont.:
7. Make gentle Dots- now go up and down on the paper, now back and forth across the paper.
8. Put one arm and hand over the other and make a Big X and now move the other arm and hand on top, now the other on top (repeat 4-5 times)
9. Make Fast Circles, go around really fast, now gradually slower and smaller, until you have a small circle add dot in the middle of the smallest circle, and STOP.

B. Bi-Lateral Drawing:
Flip paper and re-tape paper to table
With markers in each hand children are instructed to:
1. Draw a waterline
2. Draw a boat (can be a traditional boat of particular population and add cultural teachings)
3. Draw a motor or sails to the boat (if applicable)
4. Draw a flag (of particular people)
5. Draw someone fishing with a line in the water with a hook
6. Draw some fish in the water
7. Add a shark

MOTIVATION: "We all have problems in our lives. Today we are going to solve a small problem that you may have in your life. It could be a problem like losing your homework, or missing the bus."

C. Solve A Problem
1. Have the children fold paper in half, then half again, then half again- you will end up with little boxes creased on the paper.
2. Draw a problem in the first square.
3. In the next square draw a step the child took to begin to solve the problem.
4. Draw in separate squares all the steps it took to solve the problem.
5. Sharing images with class may not be appropriate as children may have drawn emotionally disturbing problems. It may be best not to share with peers.
6. Ask each child to look at their own images.

CLOSURE/ DISCUSSION

- Was it hard or easy to solve the problem?

- How many steps did it take to solve it?

- Did you solve it in a negative or positive way?

- If you didn't solve it in a positive way, how could you solve it in a positive way?

- Did you solve it by yourself or with others?

- If you didn't solved it with others, how could you have asked for help?

Facilitator Manual Start Up! 97

WEEK 12 — DRAW YOURSELF IN YOUR FAVORITE SEASON

PROBLEM PHASE

Purpose:
Emotional Homeostasis

Goal:
Exploration of Feelings and Perceptions

Neural Activity:
Limbic

Benefits:
- Emotional Identification
- Emotional Expression
- Self Disclosure

Duration:
12 Weeks

Session 2 - Friday

ACTIVITY: DRAW YOURSELF IN YOUR FAVORITE SEASON

Art Materials:
- Markers
- 2 Pieces each of 9 x 12 paper
- Oil Pastels

HEAD SHOULDERS KNEES & TOES

BREATHING / MEDITATION
"Close your eyes and breathe deeply. Think about a difficult emotion you may have. Imagine it is your favorite time of the year and you go outside to connect with nature to help you work through this difficult emotion. If it is winter, you may choose to build a snowman or throw snowballs at a wall, or if it's spring you may decide to pick flowers or walk barefoot through the rain. If it's summer, you may choose to ride a horse, go for a swim or ride your bike. If it is Fall, you may collect leaves and jump into them. There are many things to do in nature during every season. What do you like to do that makes you feel better? Imagine this and take 3 deep breaths."

ART DIRECTIVES:

A. Bi-Lateral Scribble:
Two handed Marker drawing (1 Marker/crayon for each hand): Each movement is done for 9-10 seconds. We encourage the children to look at their marks on the paper, the teacher can stand at the front of the group and demonstrate on the chalkboard, describing the process of bilateral scribbling **(Younger children may need help with taping and movements at first):**

1. Tape Paper onto table (horizontally).
2. Make Random Marks with both hands.
3. Make Vertical Lines beginning from the bottom of the paper to the top, up and down. (can alternate hands).
4. Make Horizontal Lines, across paper with each hand on opposite edge of page," bringing their markers to meet in the middle. Have children cross the midline (cross arms to opposite sides of the paper and back to opposite side of page-repeat)
5. Make two Arcs, or windshield wiper movements, back and forth. Let the Arcs move into two large circles and go around and around.
6. Continue to make Circles in the reverse direction,- reverse again/ repeating.

Start Up! — Facilitator Manual

DRAW YOURSELF IN YOUR FAVORITE SEASON

WEEK 12

A. Bi-Lateral Scribble Cont.:
7. Make gentle Dots- now go up and down on the paper, now back and forth across the paper.
8. Put one arm and hand over the other and make a Big X and now move the other arm and hand on top, now the other on top (repeat 4-5 times)
9. Make Fast Circles, go around really fast, now gradually slower and smaller, until you have a small circle add dot in the middle of the smallest circle, and STOP.

B. Bi-Lateral Drawing:
Flip paper and re-tape paper to table
With markers in each hand children are instructed to:
1. Draw a groundline
2. Draw a desert
3. Draw a cactus
4. Draw a tumbleweed
5. Draw a lizard
6. Draw a big rock
7. Draw a vulture in the sky

MOTIVATION: "There are four seasons of the year. There are different things we like to do in each season. In winter you might like to ski or build snowmen. In summer you might like to swim, or camp. You might like one season more than others. Today we are going to draw a picture of yourself in your favorite season."

C. Draw Yourself In Your Favorite Season
1. Have children draw themselves doing something they enjoy during their favorite season.
2. Ask if anyone would like to share.

CLOSURE/DISCUSSION

- What it hard to pick a favorite season or easy?

- What did you like most about this activity?

- What did you like least about this activity?

- What did you learn about yourself today?

Facilitator Manual Start Up! 99

Congratulations!

You have completed the Problem Phase, completing the second 12 weeks of START UP!

You can decide if your class is ready to jump to the Transformation Phase, or you can choose to start over in the Self Phase or repeat the Problem Phase. Remember: repetition reinforces, strengthens, and re-builds neural pathways, so it doesn't hurt to repeat activities.

Readiness to move to the Transformation Phase is indicated by:

- Ability to maintain improvements in behavior (although there may be movement forward with intermittent regression)
- Ability to access and tolerate affect (feeling or emotion)
- Ability and comfort in talking about art making
- Ability to have meaningful relationships

THE TRANSFORMATION PHASE - 8 weeks

The following activities are designed to offer children safe and enjoyable activities that will promote development.

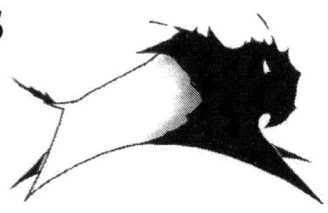

Objective

Whereas the Self Phase was focused on physical homeostasis, and the Problem Phase was centered on emotional homeostasis, the Transformation Phase is focused on cognitive homeostasis, and the ability to possess a cognitive understanding of the past and utilize cognitive-driven behavior. Behavior becomes less impulsive and more deliberate with the ability to engage the frontal cortex. Evidence that a child or adolescent has begun to more fully engage this part of the brain is demonstrated in understanding the difference between right and wrong (judgment); understanding consequences of actions; demonstrating the capacity to problem-solve; and developing empathy; compassion; and wisdom. Transforming traumatic reactivity in maladaptive coping mechanisms and behaviors, and instilling positive and appropriate, solution-oriented coping mechanisms governed by intact moral judgment is the goal of the Transformation Phase.

The cerebrum, is the largest part of the human brain, associated with higher brain function such as thought and action. The cerebral cortex is divided into four sections, called "lobes": the frontal lobe, parietal lobe, occipital lobe, and temporal lobe. Because the frontal lobe is part of the cerebrum structure, it can begin to be accessed easier than when the child was limited to the cerebellum, and the limbic structure.

This Phase is also a period of integrating fragmented parts of the Self for reclamation and revitalization, and understanding and developing a moral imperative (Chapman, 2014). The Transformation Phase is often a time of reduced symptoms and honesty about their gains and continued struggles; there is a movement forward. Some revert to earlier maladaptive behaviors: drugs, alcohol, etc. One of the goals of the Transformation Phase is to have a child/adolescent be able to identify a behavior problem and make conscious choices to improve behavior on their own accord.

To aid in the process of transformation, opportunities for transformational art experiences are the focus of the Transformation Phase segment of the Start Up! curriculum. A mental representation is created that change *can* occur; change can occur in the classroom, and change can occur with the help of others.

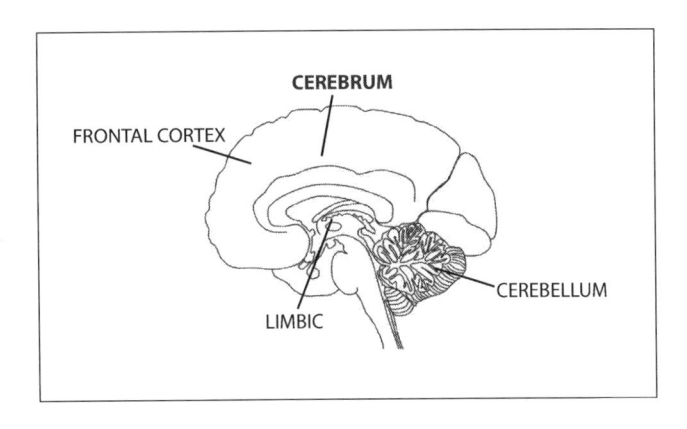

WEEK 1

CONTAINER OF TOOLS

TRANSFORMATION PHASE

Purpose:
Cognitive Homeostasis

Goal:
Understanding Past/Present and Reclaiming Self

Neural Activity:
Cerebrum

Benefits:
- Broaden Repertoire of Intellectual Concepts
- Identity Formation
- Future Orientation
- Opportunity for Choices
- Promotes Critical Thinking

Duration:
8 Weeks

Session 1 - Monday

ACTIVITY: CONTAINER OF TOOLS

Art Materials:
- Markers, (2 for each child)
- 2 Pieces each of 9x12 paper
- Construction Paper
- Scissors
- Gluesticks

SIMON SAYS

BREATHING / MEDITATION
"Close your eyes or leave them open if you really need to. Breathe in deeply through your nose or mouth, until your lungs are full. Let your breath out until your lungs are empty. With your eyes closed, imagine a path in front of you. Start to walk down this path. You come to a place on your path which represents your past. You feel accepting of your past and continue to walk forward. You come to a place on the path representing the present, what is happening currently for you. You feel accepting of your current time, feeling strong and ready for anything. Now you continue forward on the path and come to your future. Where are you? What do you see? You feel confident and powerful, like you can make anything happen for yourself knowing that your power animal and ancestors are there guiding you."

ART DIRECTIVES:
 A. Bi-Lateral Scribble:

   Two handed Marker drawing (1 Marker/crayon for each hand): Each movement is done for 9-10 seconds. We encourage the children to look at their marks on the paper, the teacher can stand at the front of the group and demonstrate on the chalkboard, describing the process of bilateral scribbling **(Younger children may need help with taping and movements at first):**
  1. Tape Paper onto table (horizontally).
  2. Make Random Marks with both hands.
  3. Make Vertical Lines beginning from the bottom of the paper to the top, up and down. (can alternate hands).
  4. Make Horizontal Lines, across paper with each hand on opposite edge of page," bringing their markers to meet in the middle. Have children cross the midline (cross arms to opposite sides of the paper and back to opposite side of page-repeat)
  5. Make two Arcs, or windshield wiper movements, back and forth. Let the Arcs move into two large circles and go around and around.

CONTAINER OF TOOLS

WEEK 1

A. Bi-Lateral Scribble Cont.:
6. Continue to make Circles in the reverse direction,- reverse again/ repeating.
7. Make gentle Dots- now go up and down on the paper, now back and forth across the paper.
8. Put one arm and hand over the other and make a Big X and now move the other arm and hand on top, now the other on top (repeat 4-5 times)
9. Make Fast Circles, go around really fast, now gradually slower and smaller, until you have a small circle add dot in the middle of the smallest circle, and STOP.

B. Bi-Lateral Drawing:
Flip paper and re-tape paper to table
With markers in each hand children are instructed to:
1. Draw a groundline
2. Draw a house with windows and door (tipi, wigwam, hut, traditional home, can add cultural teachings about traditional homes of particular population)
3. Draw a tree
4. Draw a basket of apples underneath the tree (or can be traditional food and add cultural teachings about the traditional foods of particular population)
5. Put clouds up in the sky
6. Sun / Birds

MOTIVATION: "We all have to grow up and become adults. The path to becoming an adult is not always easy. We all have to learn tools along the way to get us through life. Today you are going to choose some tools that will help you get through life."

C. Container of Tools
1. Cut paper in the shape of a 5 gallon bucket (you can choose to cut in the shape of clay/wood bowl, bark bowls, buffalo bladder bags or other object that was used to carry things in the cultural traditions of children you are working with- you can also add cultural teachings about these objects).
2. Have children cut out symbols to represent their tools to get them through life: job, money, house, friends, etc.
3. Have children prioritize items in terms of what is most important.
4. Put tools inside container (can glue them if you choose).

CLOSURE/ DISCUSSION

- What tool is most important for you?

- What tool is least important?

- Which ones you can do by yourself?

- Which ones require others?

Facilitator Manual — Start Up!

WEEK 1

DESIGN YOUR OWN BOOK COVER

TRANSFORMATION PHASE

Purpose:
Cognitive Homeostasis

Goal:
Understanding Past/Present and Reclaiming Self

Neural Activity:
Cerebrum

Benefits:
- Identity Formation
- Broaden Repertoire of Intellectual Concepts
- Future Orientation

Duration:
8 Weeks

Session 2 - Friday

ACTIVITY: DESIGN YOUR OWN BOOK COVER

Art Materials:
- Markers
- 2 Pieces of 9 x 12 paper
- Oil/Chalk Pastels
- Colored pencils

HEAD/SHOULDER/KNEES & TOES

BREATHING / MEDITATION

"Close your eyes or leave them open if you would like. Breathe in deeply through your nose or mouth, until your lungs are full. Let your breath out until your lungs are empty. Sit comfortably, feel feet on the ground. Children have a lot of people telling them what to do; parents, teachers, babysitters. Get in touch with that part of yourself who knows how to take care of yourself. Get in touch with your inner advisor or inner healer, what would that part of yourself say to you?"

ART DIRECTIVES:

A. Bi-Lateral Scribble:

Two handed Marker drawing (1 Marker/crayon for each hand): Each movement is done for 9-10 seconds. We encourage the children to look at their marks on the paper, the teacher can stand at the front of the group and demonstrate on the chalkboard, describing the process of bilateral scribbling **(Younger children may need help with taping and movements at first):**

1. Tape Paper onto table (horizontally).
2. Make Random Marks with both hands.
3. Make Vertical Lines beginning from the bottom of the paper to the top, up and down. (can alternate hands).
4. Make Horizontal Lines, across paper with each hand on opposite edge of page," bringing their markers to meet in the middle. Have children cross the midline (cross arms to opposite sides of the paper and back to opposite side of page-repeat)
5. Make two Arcs, or windshield wiper movements, back and forth. Let the Arcs move into two large circles and go around and around.
6. Continue to make Circles in the reverse direction,- reverse again/repeating.

DESIGN YOUR OWN BOOK COVER

WEEK 1

A. Bi-Lateral Scribble Cont.:
7. Make gentle Dots- now go up and down on the paper, now back and forth across the paper.
8. Put one arm and hand over the other and make a Big X and now move the other arm and hand on top, now the other on top (repeat 4-5 times)
9. Make Fast Circles, go around really fast, now gradually slower and smaller, until you have a small circle add dot in the middle of the smallest circle, and STOP.

B. Bi-Lateral Drawing Cont.:
Flip paper and re-tape paper to table
With markers in each hand children are instructed to:
1. Draw a starry sky
2. Draw some star people (can add cultural teachings about traditional star knowledge beliefs of particular population)
3. Draw a spaceship
4. Draw a moon

C. Scribble Chase
1. Select a partner (each child has 1 marker)
2. Determine who will be the leader, the follower
3. Say "GO" and the leader leads with the marker and the follower tries to follow the leader on the paper with their marker (30-40 seconds each turn)
4. Switch roles

MOTIVATION: "Imagine if you could do something really amazing in this world, what might it be? What would you hope your life would look like when you got old and someone wrote a book about you about how you did something fantastic in your life. It could be something you did for your people, or for the whole world. It could be something that your grandchildren will remember you for. Today we are going to design our own book covers of a book that someone wrote about you."

D. Design your Own Book Cover
1. Have children fold paper in half like a book cover.
2. Children can decorate their book cover based on the great deeds they did in their lives.
3. Share with the class.

CLOSURE/ DISCUSSION

- Notice if the main theme is symbols or words.

- How does that relate to your life today?

- What did you learn about yourself today?

Facilitator Manual — Start Up! — 105

WEEK 2   MAKE AN ADVERTISEMENT FOR YOURSELF

TRANSFORMATION PHASE

Purpose:
Cognitive Homeostasis

Goal:
Understanding Past/Present and Reclaiming Self

Neural Activity:
Cerebrum

Benefits:
• Self-Recognition
• Identity Formation
• Building Self-Esteem

Duration:
8 Weeks

Session 1 - Monday

ACTIVITY: MAKE AN ADVERTISEMENT FOR YOURSELF

Art Materials:
• Markers
• 2 Pieces of 9x12 paper
• Oil Pastels
• Colored Pencils

MUSIC FREEZE

BREATHING / MEDITATION
"Close your eyes or leave them open if you would like. Breathe in deeply through your nose or mouth, until your lungs are full. Let your breath out until your lungs are empty. Sit comfortably, feel your feet on the ground. Imagine you are a leader and you leading your class up a mountain. The mountain is steep and everyone is tired. You are leading the line of classmates and cheering everyone on to keep going: what are you saying to them? You allow everyone to take a break and give them a snack. What do you give them? You finally get to the top and reward the class by giving them something. What do you give them? Then imagine going back down the mountain. When you get to the bottom you can gently open your eyes."

ART DIRECTIVES:
 A. Bi-Lateral Scribble:
   Two handed Marker drawing (1 Marker/crayon for each hand): Each movement is done for 9-10 seconds. We encourage the children to look at their marks on the paper, the teacher can stand at the front of the group and demonstrate on the chalkboard, describing the process of bilateral scribbling **(Younger children may need help with taping and movements at first):**
  1. Tape Paper onto table (horizontally).
  2. Make Random Marks with both hands.
  3. Make Vertical Lines beginning from the bottom of the paper to the top, up and down. (can alternate hands).
  4. Make Horizontal Lines, across paper with each hand on opposite edge of page," bringing their markers to meet in the middle. Have children cross the midline (cross arms to opposite sides of the paper and back to opposite side of page-repeat)
  5. Make two Arcs, or windshield wiper movements, back and forth. Let the Arcs move into two large circles and go around and around.
  6. Continue to make Circles in the reverse direction,- reverse again/ repeating.

MAKE AN ADVERTISEMENT FOR YOURSELF

WEEK 2

A. Bi-Lateral Scribble Cont.:
7. Make gentle Dots- now go up and down on the paper, now back and forth across the paper.
8. Put one arm and hand over the other and make a Big X and now move the other arm and hand on top, now the other on top (repeat 4-5 times)
9. Make Fast Circles, go around really fast, now gradually slower and smaller, until you have a small circle add dot in the middle of the smallest circle, and STOP.

B. Bi-Lateral Drawing:
Flip paper and re-tape paper to table
With markers in each hand children are instructed to:
1. Draw a waterline
2. Draw a boat (can be a traditional boat of particular population and add cultural teachings)
3. Draw a motor or sails to the boat (if applicable)
4. Draw a flag
5. Draw someone fishing with a line in the water with a hook
6. Draw some fish in the water
7. Add a shark
8. Draw a starfish in the water
9. Add clouds/sun/birds
10. TEACHER- If you are a people originated near water, include cultural traditions and stories of water.

MOTIVATION: "What is an advertisement? Everyone is good at something. It might be sports, music, writing, helping others, etc. Think about something you are good at. Today you are going to make an advertisement, advertising to others what you are good at."

C. Make an Advertisement For Yourself
1. "What do you do well that you would advertise about yourself?"
2. Make a poster that advertises what you are good at.
3. **Teacher: If the child cannot think of anything he/she is good at, give the option of advertising something they want to be good at.**
4. Share with class.

CLOSURE/ DISCUSSION

- What was easy?
- What was hard?
- What did you learn about yourself today?

WEEK 2   DRAW A BRIDGE

TRANSFORMATION PHASE

Purpose:
Cognitive Homeostasis

Goal:
Understanding Past/Present and Reclaiming Self

Neural Activity:
Cerebrum

Benefits:
- Installation of Hope
- Future Orientation
- Delaying Gratification
- Identity Formation
- Acknowledging the Past

Duration:
8 Weeks

Session 2, Friday

ACTIVITY: DRAW A BRIDGE

Art Materials:
- Markers
- Largest paper for the desk space
- 2 Pieces of 9x12 paper
- Colored Pencils

SIMON SAYS

BREATHING / MEDITATION
"Close your eyes or leave them open if you really need to. Breathe in deeply through your nose or mouth, until your lungs are full. Let your breath out until your lungs are empty." Do this 3 times, or as many times as tolerated. Can set a timer for longer and longer times, up to 3-5 minutes.

ART DIRECTIVES:
A. Bi-Lateral Scribble:
   Two handed Marker drawing (1 Marker/crayon for each hand): Each movement is done for 9-10 seconds. We encourage the children to look at their marks on the paper, the teacher can stand at the front of the group and demonstrate on the chalkboard, describing the process of bilateral scribbling **(Younger children may need help with taping and movements at first):**
1. Tape Paper onto table (horizontally).
2. Make Random Marks with both hands.
3. Make Vertical Lines beginning from the bottom of the paper to the top, up and down. (can alternate hands).
4. Make Horizontal Lines, across paper with each hand on opposite edge of page," bringing their markers to meet in the middle. Have children cross the midline (cross arms to opposite sides of the paper and back to opposite side of page-repeat)
5. Make two Arcs, or windshield wiper movements, back and forth. Let the Arcs move into two large circles and go around and around.
6. Continue to make Circles in the reverse direction,- reverse again/ repeating.
7. Make gentle Dots- now go up and down on the paper, now back and forth across the paper.
8. Put one arm and hand over the other and make a Big X and now move the other arm and hand on top, now the other on top (repeat 4-5 times)
9. Make Fast Circles, go around really fast, now gradually slower and smaller, until you have a small circle add dot in the middle of the smallest circle, and STOP.

Start Up!   Facilitator Manual

DRAW A BRIDGE

WEEK 2

B. Bi-Lateral Drawing:
Flip paper and re-tape paper to table.
With markers in each hand children are instructed to:
1. Draw underground
2. Draw a snake underground
3. Draw a family of snakes underground
4. Draw a prairie dog underground
5. Draw a fox
6. Draw a rabbit
7. Add a family of rabbits
8. Draw some ants
9. Add clouds/sun/birds above ground

MOTIVATION: "Bridges are helpful to bring us from one place to another. They help us cross rivers, oceans, and valleys. There are many types of bridges. Some cultures in the old days used logs or rope bridges to cross by foot. Today big fancy bridges help vehicles to cross to get to where they need to go. Bridges take us from one place to another place. Today you are going to think about where you have been in your past and where you would like to go in your future."

C. Draw A Bridge
1. Place paper horizontally on your desk.
2. Think of your past or where you were a year ago. Draw your past on the left side of the paper.
3. Think about the goals you have for your future. Your goals can be anything you can imagine. Dream Big! Draw these goals on the right side of the paper.
4. Draw a bridge in the middle; between the past and future. It can be a bridge from your culture, or any culture. It can be a famous bridge or one from your own town or city.
5. Think about where you are in your life in relation to your past and your future that you have drawn. Draw yourself somewhere on your bridge according to where you are at in your life.
6. Can play soft traditional music in background
7. **Teacher: " You can do anything you want to do in life. Where are you on your bridge? You need to believe in yourself. You just need to work at it and I am here to support you." Encourage children to think about their futures and to work hard to get to the other side of the bridge to get to their future goals. Save the Draw a Bridge drawings and repeat at the end of the school year so children can see themselves moving forward in order to compare and contrast progress.**

CLOSURE/ DISCUSSION

- Where did you start and where are you headed?

- Where are you on the bridge?

- What did you learn about yourself today?

Facilitator Manual　　　Start Up!　　　109

WEEK 3
FAMILY OF ANIMALS

TRANSFORMATION PHASE

Purpose:
Cognitive Homeostasis

Goal:
Understanding Past/Present and Reclaiming Self

Neural Activity:
Cerebrum

Benefits:
- Delaying gratification
- Patience
- Broadening repertoire of Intellectual Concepts

Duration:
8 Weeks

Session 1 - Monday

ACTIVITY: FAMILY OF ANIMALS

Art Materials:
- Markers
- Largest paper for the desk space
- 1 Piece each of 9x12 paper
- Model Magic Clay- 2 pkg each

HEAD SHOULDERS KNEES AND TOES

BREATHING / MEDITATION
"Close your eyes or leave them open if you would like. Breathe in deeply through your nose or mouth, until your lungs are full. Let your breath out until your lungs are empty. Sit comfortably, feel your feet on the ground. Imagine you are living back in the old times before grocery stores and you needed to hunt for food. Think of the food that your ancestors ate. It might be buffalo, sheep, pig, fish, whale, antelope, etc. Imagine yourself hunting for your traditional food. After you get the animal imagine how you would divide it among your people, and how you would prepare it."

ART DIRECTIVES:
A. Bi-Lateral Scribble:
   Two handed Marker drawing (1 Marker/crayon for each hand): Each movement is done for 9-10 seconds. We encourage the children to look at their marks on the paper, the teacher can stand at the front of the group and demonstrate on the chalkboard, describing the process of bilateral scribbling **(Younger children may need help with taping and movements at first):**
  1. Tape Paper onto table (horizontally).
  2. Make Random Marks with both hands.
  3. Make Vertical Lines beginning from the bottom of the paper to the top, up and down. (can alternate hands).
  4. Make Horizontal Lines, across paper with each hand on opposite edge of page," bringing their markers to meet in the middle. Have children cross the midline (cross arms to opposite sides of the paper and back to opposite side of page-repeat)
  5. Make two Arcs, or windshield wiper movements, back and forth. Let the Arcs move into two large circles and go around and around.
  6. Continue to make Circles in the reverse direction,- reverse again/ repeating.

Start Up!

FAMILY OF ANIMALS

WEEK 3

A. Bi-Lateral Scribble Cont.:
7. Make gentle Dots- now go up and down on the paper, now back and forth across the paper.
8. Put one arm and hand over the other and make a Big X and now move the other arm and hand on top, now the other on top (repeat 4-5 times)
9. Make Fast Circles, go around really fast, now gradually slower and smaller, until you have a small circle add dot in the middle of the smallest circle, and STOP.

B. Bi-Lateral Drawing:
Flip paper and re-tape paper to table
With markers in each hand children are instructed to:
1. Draw a groundline
2. Draw a dinosaur (or animal special to traditions of particular population, buffalo, whale, jaguar, etc. Include cultural teachings of animal)
3. Draw tree
4. Draw a sun
5. Draw another animal

MOTIVATION: "Many species have families; ducks, rabbits, birds, tigers, deer, and humans. Today we are going to make a family of animals with clay."

C. Family Of Animals - Scupture
1. Have children choose a kind of animal they would like to sculpt. It can be an animal that is scared to their culture: buffalo, jaguar, whale, giraffe, horse, etc. (You can tell cultural history of different animals.)
2. Have children open the model magic clay and start to sculpt their animal family of choice. Dry the animal sculptures labeled and in a safe place for next session.
3. **Teacher: Often when children do artwork about families of animals, subconscious material about their own families may be elicited. Notice children's responses.**

CLOSURE/ DISCUSSION

- Was it hard or easy to do this?

- (Let children know that if it was a struggle it is ok to talk about it)

- Do animals have names or does the family have a family name?

WEEK 3

FAMILY OF ANIMALS - continued

TRANSFORMATION PHASE

Purpose:
Cognitive Homeostasis

Goal:
Understanding Past/Present and Reclaiming Self

Neural Activity:
Cerebrum

Benefits:
• Broadening repertoire of Intellectual Concepts
• Development of Imagination
• Eye-hand Coordination
• Delaying Gratification
• Patience

Duration:
8 Weeks

Session 2 - Friday

ACTIVITY: FAMILY OF ANIMALS - continued

Art Materials:
• Markers
• Largest paper for the desk space
• 1 Piece each of 9x12 paper
• Acrylic Paint in sm. Cups
• Paint Brushes- Various Sized
• Construction paper
• Scissors
• Tape

MUSIC FREEZE

BREATHING / MEDITATION
"Close your eyes or leave them open if you really need to. Breathe in deeply through your nose or mouth, until your lungs are full. Let your breath out until your lungs are empty. Sit comfortably, feel feet on the ground. Breathe in and imagine a white light filling your body. Let it out. Imagine a color that represents your stress. Where in your body is this stress color? Breathe in the white light and let it take over your stress. Breathe out the stress color. Breathe in white light into your entire body, from your toes to the top of your head

ART DIRECTIVES:
 A. Bi-Lateral Scribble:
   Two handed Marker drawing (1 Marker/crayon for each hand): Each movement is done for 9-10 seconds. We encourage the children to look at their marks on the paper, the teacher can stand at the front of the group and demonstrate on the chalkboard, describing the process of bilateral scribbling **(Younger children may need help with taping and movements at first):**
  1. Tape Paper onto table (horizontally).
  2. Make Random Marks with both hands.
  3. Make Vertical Lines beginning from the bottom of the paper to the top, up and down. (can alternate hands).
  4. Make Horizontal Lines, across paper with each hand on opposite edge of page," bringing their markers to meet in the middle. Have children cross the midline (cross arms to opposite sides of the paper and back to opposite side of page-repeat)
  5. Make two Arcs, or windshield wiper movements, back and forth. Let the Arcs move into two large circles and go around and around.

Start Up! Facilitator Manual

FAMILY OF ANIMALS - continued

WEEK 3

A. Bi-Lateral Scribble Cont.:
6. Continue to make Circles in the reverse direction,- reverse again/repeating.
7. Make gentle Dots- now go up and down on the paper, now back and forth across the paper.
8. Put one arm and hand over the other and make a Big X and now move the other arm and hand on top, now the other on top (repeat 4-5 times)
9. Make Fast Circles, go around really fast, now gradually slower and smaller, until you have a small circle add dot in the middle of the smallest circle, and STOP.

B. Bi-Lateral Drawing:
Flip paper and re-tape paper to table
With markers in each hand children are instructed to:
1. Draw a groundline
2. Draw a desert
3. Draw a cactus
4. Draw a tumbleweed
5. Draw a lizard
6. Draw a big rock
7. Draw a vulture in the sky
8. Teacher- You can include traditions and stories of Desert Tribes; diet, how they obtained water, etc

MOTIVATION: "Remember the animal families we made earlier this week? Today we are going to paint them and make a home for them."

C. Family Of Animals - continued
1. Have children paint their animal families using acrylic paint in small cups and various sized brushes.
2. Have children think about what the animal family need to survive.
3. Have children cut out shapes representing objects of what the family will need to live. They can use to tape to construct things with the construction paper.
4. **Teacher: Notice the responses of the children as this may elicit emotions about their own family.**

CLOSURE/ DISCUSSION

- Was this easy or hard?

- What did your animal family need most?

- What did your animal family need least?

Facilitator Manual — Start Up!

WEEK 4

FAMILY OF ANIMALS - continued

TRANSFORMATION PHASE

Purpose:
Cognitive Homeostasis

Goal:
Understanding Past/Present and Reclaiming Self

Neural Activity:
Cerebrum

Benefits:
- Development of Abstract Thinking
- Identity Formation
- Delaying Gratification
- Patience
- Broadening Repertoire of Intellectual Concepts

Duration:
8 Weeks

Session 1 - Monday

ACTIVITY: FAMILY OF ANIMALS - continued

Art Materials:
- Markers
- Largest paper for the desk space
- 1 Piece each of 9x12 paper
- Construction paper
- Scissors
- Tape
- Glue
- Cardboard

SIMON SAYS

BREATHING / MEDITATION
"Close your eyes or leave them open if you really need to. Breathe in deeply through your nose or mouth, until your lungs are full. Let your breath out until your lungs are empty." Do this 3 times, or as many times as tolerated.

ART DIRECTIVES:
 A. Bi-Lateral Scribble:
   Two handed Marker drawing (1 Marker/crayon for each hand): Each movement is done for 9-10 seconds. We encourage the children to look at their marks on the paper, the teacher can stand at the front of the group and demonstrate on the chalkboard, describing the process of bilateral scribbling **(Younger children may need help with taping and movements at first):**
  1. Tape Paper onto table (horizontally).
  2. Make Random Marks with both hands.
  3. Make Vertical Lines beginning from the bottom of the paper to the top, up and down. (can alternate hands).
  4. Make Horizontal Lines, across paper with each hand on opposite edge of page," bringing their markers to meet in the middle. Have children cross the midline (cross arms to opposite sides of the paper and back to opposite side of page-repeat)
  5. Make two Arcs, or windshield wiper movements, back and forth. Let the Arcs move into two large circles and go around and around.

Start Up! — Facilitator Manual

FAMILY OF ANIMALS - continued

WEEK 4

A. Bi-Lateral Scribble Cont.:
7. "When I say GO- make gentle Dots- now go up and down on the paper, now back and forth across the paper, until I say STOP."
8. "When I say GO- put one arm and hand over the other and make a Big X and now move the other arm and hand on top, now the other on top (repeat 4-5 times) until I say STOP".
9. "When I say GO- make Fast Circles, go around really fast, now gradually slower and smaller, until you have a small circle add dot in the middle of the smallest circle, and STOP.

B. Bi-Lateral Drawing:
Flip paper and re-tape paper to table
With markers in each hand children are instructed to:
1. Draw a groundline
2. Draw favorite animal
3. Draw tree
4. Draw a sun
5. Draw another animal of same type

MOTIVATION: "Last time we made animal families and painted them, and made some things for them that they would need to survive. Today we are going to make a home for them and place them in their home along with the things they need."

C. Family Of Animals - continued
1. **Teacher: "What kinds of things will your animal family need to live? What kind of home do they live in? What kind of environment do they live in?"**
2. Ask the children to make a scene of their animal family's home.
3. Have children glue colored construction paper on top of a piece of cardboard.
4. Placing all the objects the animal family will need to survive within the scene.

CLOSURE/ DISCUSSION

- What do you think the animals would say about where they live?

- What do you think it would be like to live there?

- What is a typical day in this environment

Facilitator Manual — Start Up! — 115

WEEK 4

POSITIVE COPING SKILLS

TRANSFORMATION PHASE

Purpose:
Cognitive Homeostasis

Goal:
Understanding Past/Present and Reclaiming Self

Neural Activity:
Cerebrum

Benefits:
- Normalize Emotions
- Community Building
- Learning Adaptive Coping Strategies
- Development of Abstract Thinking
- Emotional Regulation
- Emotional Identification
- Emotional Expression

Duration:
8 Weeks

Session 2 - Friday

ACTIVITY: POSITIVE COPING SKILLS

Art Materials:
- Markers, (2 for each child)
- 2 Pieces each of 9x12 paper
- Oil pastels

HEAD SHOULDERS KNEES & TOES

BREATHING / MEDITATION

"Close your eyes or leave them open if you would like. Breathe in deeply through your nose or mouth, until your lungs are full. Let your breath out until your lungs are empty. Imagine yourself feeling a difficult emotion or feeling. Imagine that difficult emotion or feeling as a color. Imagine that color draining out of your body through your feet and going into the earth, letting this difficult emotion or feeling go. You do not have to hold onto it. Now imagine a happy feeling and imagine it as a color filling your entire body up. You feel warm and safe. Let's take 4 deep breaths and fill our bodies with this happy feeling."

ART DIRECTIVES:

A. Bi-Lateral Scribble:

Two handed Marker drawing (1 Marker/crayon for each hand): Each movement is done for 9-10 seconds. We encourage the children to look at their marks on the paper, the teacher can stand at the front of the group and demonstrate on the chalkboard, describing the process of bilateral scribbling **(Younger children may need help with taping and movements at first):**

1. Tape Paper onto table (horizontally).
2. Make Random Marks with both hands.
3. Make Vertical Lines beginning from the bottom of the paper to the top, up and down. (can alternate hands).
4. Make Horizontal Lines, across paper with each hand on opposite edge of page," bringing their markers to meet in the middle. Have children cross the midline (cross arms to opposite sides of the paper and back to opposite side of page-repeat)
5. Make two Arcs, or windshield wiper movements, back and forth. Let the Arcs move into two large circles and go around and around.
6. Continue to make Circles in the reverse direction,- reverse again/ repeating.

Start Up!   Facilitator Manual

POSITIVE COPING SKILLS

WEEK 4

A. Bi-Lateral Scribble Cont.:
7. Make gentle Dots- now go up and down on the paper, now back and forth across the paper.
8. Put one arm and hand over the other and make a Big X and now move the other arm and hand on top, now the other on top (repeat 4-5 times)
9. Make Fast Circles, go around really fast, now gradually slower and smaller, until you have a small circle add dot in the middle of the smallest circle, and STOP.

B. Bi-Lateral Drawing:
Flip paper and re-tape paper to table
With markers in each hand children are instructed to:
1. Draw a sky
2. Draw a moon
3. Draw stars
4. Draw planets
5. Draw a spaceship
6. Draw a star being (alien)

MOTIVATION: "There are many kinds of emotions and there are many ways in which we handle these emotions. Today we are going to explore four different emotions and some positive ways we can cope with or handle these emotions."

C. Positive Coping Skills
1. Have children fold paper in half, then in half again, making creases in the paper showing 4 squares.
2. We are going to focus on the emotions: happy, mad, frustrated, lonely.
3. Label each square with one emotion: happy, mad, frustrated, lonely.
4. Make a symbol for each emotion in the appropriate box (example: for mad; child might draw sharp teeth).
5. On back of paper in appropriate box- write down/or draw what you do to cope in a positive way (example: for mad-; "I go outside and yell")
6. Share with Class: Have a child share a coping skill while standing, have everyone who also does this coping skill raise their hand.
7. Have another child share another coping skill while standing, have everyone who also does this coping skill raise their hand.
8. Repeat.
9. **Teacher: Burn sage, copal, palo santo, etc. to purify children's emotions. Save these drawings for next session.**

CLOSURE/ DISCUSSION

- How do you feel when you cope with your emotions in that way?

- What did you learn about yourself today?

Facilitator Manual — Start Up!

WEEK 5

NEGATIVE COPING SKILLS

TRANSFORMATION PHASE

Purpose:
Cognitive Homeostasis

Goal:
Understanding Past/Present and Reclaiming Self

Neural Activity:
Cerebrum

Benefits:
• Normalize Emotions
• Community Building
• Learning Adaptive Coping Strategies
• Development of Abstract Thinking
• Emotional Regulation
• Emotional Identification
• Emotional Expression
• Transforming negative to positive

Duration:
8 Weeks

Session 1 - Monday

ACTIVITY: NEGATIVE COPING SKILLS

Art Materials:
• Markers
• 2 Pieces each of 9x12 paper
• Oil Pastels

HEAD SHOULDERS KNEES &TOES

BREATHING / MEDITATION
"Close your eyes or leave them open if you would like. Breathe in deeply through your nose or mouth, until your lungs are full. Let your breath out until your lungs are empty. Imagine yourself feeling a difficult emotion or feeling. Imagine that difficult emotion or feeling as a color. Imagine that color draining out of your body through your feet and going into the earth, letting this difficult emotion or feeling go. You do not have to hold onto it. Now imagine a happy feeling and imagine it as a color filling your entire body up. You feel warm and safe. Let's take 4 deep breaths and fill our bodies with this happy feeling."

ART DIRECTIVES:
  A. Bi-Lateral Scribble:
   Two handed Marker drawing (1 Marker/crayon for each hand): Each movement is done for 9-10 seconds. We encourage the children to look at their marks on the paper, the teacher can stand at the front of the group and demonstrate on the chalkboard, describing the process of bilateral scribbling **(Younger children may need help with taping and movements at first):**
  1. Tape Paper onto table (horizontally).
  2. Make Random Marks with both hands.
  3. Make Vertical Lines beginning from the bottom of the paper to the top, up and down. (can alternate hands).
  4. Make Horizontal Lines, across paper with each hand on opposite edge of page," bringing their markers to meet in the middle. Have children cross the midline (cross arms to opposite sides of the paper and back to opposite side of page-repeat)
  5. Make two Arcs, or windshield wiper movements, back and forth. Let the Arcs move into two large circles and go around and around.
  6. Continue to make Circles in the reverse direction,- reverse again/ repeating.
"

NEGATIVE COPING SKILLS

WEEK 5

A. Bi-Lateral Scribble Cont.:
7. Make gentle Dots- now go up and down on the paper, now back and forth across the paper.
8. Put one arm and hand over the other and make a Big X and now move the other arm and hand on top, now the other on top (repeat 4-5 times)
9. Make Fast Circles, go around really fast, now gradually slower and smaller, until you have a small circle add dot in the middle of the smallest circle, and STOP.

B. Bi-Lateral Drawing:
Flip paper and re-tape paper to table
With markers in each hand children are instructed to:
1. Draw a ground line
2. Draw a jungle of trees
3. Draw a monkey
4. Draw a tiger
5. Draw a river
6. Draw a parrot
7. Draw fish in the river

MOTIVATION: Teacher: Hand back the "Positive Coping Skills" drawings from last session. "Last time we explored positive coping skills for four different emotions. What were the four emotions we focused on? Do you remember how it felt when we drew the positive ways that we coped with these emotions? Today we are going to explore the negative ways we cope with these same emotions."

C. Negative Coping Skills
1. Have children fold paper in half, then in half again, making creases in the paper showing 4 squares.
2. We are going to focus on the emotions: happy, mad, frustrated, lonely.
3. Label each square with one emotion: happy, mad, frustrated, lonely.
4. Make a symbol for each emotion in the appropriate box (example: for happy; child might draw a smile).
5. On back of paper in appropriate box- write down/or draw what you do to cope in a negative way (example: for mad-; "I hit my brother.")
6. Share with Class: Have a child share a coping skill while standing, have everyone who also does this coping skill raise their hand.
7. Have another child share another coping skill while standing, have everyone who also does this coping skill raise their hand.
8. Repeat.
9. **Teacher: Burn sage, copal, palo santo, etc. to purify children's emotions.**

CLOSURE/ DISCUSSION

- How do you feel when you cope with your emotions in that way?

- What did you learn about yourself today?

Facilitator Manual   Start Up!   119

WEEK 5

CLASSROOM PROBLEM / SOLUTION

TRANSFORMATION PHASE **Purpose:** Cognitive Homeostasis **Goal:** Understanding Past/Present and Reclaiming Self **Neural Activity:** Cerebrum **Benefits:** • Transforming Negative to Positive • Team Building • Increases Problem Solving Abilities **Duration:** 8 Weeks

Session 2 - Friday

ACTIVITY: CLASSROOM PROBLEM / SOLUTION

Art Materials:
- Markers
- 1 Piece, largest paper for the desk space
- Large Craft Paper

MUSIC FREEZE

BREATHING / MEDITATION
"Close your eyes or leave them open if you really need to. Breathe in deeply through your nose or mouth, until your lungs are full. Let your breath out until your lungs are empty. Sit comfortably, feel feet on the ground. We talked about an inner advisor before; the voice inside yourself who knows how to take care of you. Imagine there is a problem in your life, a small problem like you lost your homework, etc. Imagine your inner advisor's voice telling you what you need to do to make the problem better. Thank your inner advisor for this advice."

ART DIRECTIVES:

A. Bi-Lateral Scribble:
Two handed Marker drawing (1 Marker/crayon for each hand): Each movement is done for 9-10 seconds. We encourage the children to look at their marks on the paper, the teacher can stand at the front of the group and demonstrate on the chalkboard, describing the process of bilateral scribbling **(Younger children may need help with taping and movements at first):**

1. Tape Paper onto table (horizontally).
2. Make Random Marks with both hands.
3. Make Vertical Lines beginning from the bottom of the paper to the top, up and down. (can alternate hands).
4. Make Horizontal Lines, across paper with each hand on opposite edge of page," bringing their markers to meet in the middle. Have children cross the midline (cross arms to opposite sides of the paper and back to opposite side of page-repeat)
5. Make two Arcs, or windshield wiper movements, back and forth. Let the Arcs move into two large circles and go around and around.
6. Continue to make Circles in the reverse direction,- reverse again/ repeating.

Start Up! — Facilitator Manual

CLASSROOM PROBLEM / SOLUTION

A. Bi-Lateral Scribble Cont.:
7. Make gentle Dots- now go up and down on the paper, now back and forth across the paper.
8. Put one arm and hand over the other and make a Big X and now move the other arm and hand on top, now the other on top (repeat 4-5 times)
9. Make Fast Circles, go around really fast, now gradually slower and smaller, until you have a small circle add dot in the middle of the smallest circle, and STOP.

B. Bi-Lateral Drawing:
Flip paper and re-tape paper to table
With markers in each hand children are instructed to:
1. Draw Waterline
2. Draw Mountains
3. Draw birds
4. Draw fish in the river

MOTIVATION: "There are always things that to be done at a school; repairs, projects, improvements, etc. Today, we are going to think of a repair, project or improvement we want to see at our school. We will figure out what the problem is and, together, figure out a solution."

C. Classroom Problem / Solution
1. Have the class agree on a problem or teacher picks a problem that needs to be fixed in the school that doesn't cost a lot of money; raking leaves, washing windows, build a picnic area, garden, etc.
   Example: The class wants a garden- have children figure out what materials you will need, how to get the supplies and how to fundraise for them.
2. Tape big butcher paper on a table. Draw a line down the middle and label the left side "Problem" and the right side label "Solution?
3. Have kids come up and draw on each section what they think the problem/solution will be.
4. **Teacher: How can you use our positive coping skills as a class to solve this problem? Several emotions may have come up for you during this process(frustration, negative emotions, happy emotions). Sometimes it is not always fun or easy to find solutions for a problem.**

CLOSURE/ DISCUSSION

- How does it feel to work as a member of a large team?

- What are the feelings you have about what you did?

WEEK 6

THANKFUL TO OUR ANCESTORS

TRANSFORMATION PHASE

Purpose:
Cognitive Homeostasis

Goal:
Understanding Past/Present and Reclaiming Self

Neural Activity:
Cerebrum

Benefits:
- Visual Discrimination
- Identity Formation
- Cultivating Cultural Pride/Identity

Duration:
8 Weeks

Session 1 - Monday

ACTIVITY: THANKFUL TO OUR ANCESTORS

Art Materials:
- Markers
- 1 Piece each of 9 x 12 paper
- White Chalk
- Black Paper

SIMON SAYS

BREATHING / MEDITATION
"Close your eyes or leave them open if you really need to. Breathe in deeply through your nose or mouth, until your lungs are full. Let your breath out until your lungs are empty. Sit comfortably, feel your feet on the ground. Think about a goal you have for yourself; it might be to go to college or to pass an upcoming test. Imagine your ancestors coming to you or it could be a grandfather or grandmother who is still alive. Imagine them guiding you in how to achieve this goal."

ART DIRECTIVES:
A. Bi-Lateral Scribble:
Two handed Marker drawing (1 Marker/crayon for each hand): Each movement is done for 9-10 seconds. We encourage the children to look at their marks on the paper, the teacher can stand at the front of the group and demonstrate on the chalkboard, describing the process of bilateral scribbling **(Younger children may need help with taping and movements at first):**
1. Tape Paper onto table (horizontally).
2. Make Random Marks with both hands.
3. Make Vertical Lines beginning from the bottom of the paper to the top, up and down. (can alternate hands).
4. Make Horizontal Lines, across paper with each hand on opposite edge of page," bringing their markers to meet in the middle. Have children cross the midline (cross arms to opposite sides of the paper and back to opposite side of page-repeat)
5. Make two Arcs, or windshield wiper movements, back and forth. Let the Arcs move into two large circles and go around and around.
6. Continue to make Circles in the reverse direction,- reverse again/ repeating.

THANKFUL TO OUR ANCESTORS

WEEK 6

A. Bi-Lateral Scribble Cont.:
7. Make gentle Dots- now go up and down on the paper, now back and forth across the paper.
8. Put one arm and hand over the other and make a Big X and now move the other arm and hand on top, now the other on top (repeat 4-5 times)
9. Make Fast Circles, go around really fast, now gradually slower and smaller, until you have a small circle add dot in the middle of the smallest circle, and STOP.

B. Bi-Lateral Drawing:
Flip paper and re-tape paper to table
With markers in each hand children are instructed to:
1. Draw a groundline
2. Draw a house from another culture with windows and door (tipi, wigwam, hut, traditional home, can add cultural teachings about traditional homes of particular population)
3. Draw a tree
4. Draw a basket of apples underneath the tree (or can be traditional food and add cultural teachings about the traditional foods of particular population)
5. Put clouds up in the sky
6. Sun / Birds

MOTIVATION: "Ancestors are members of our family who have lived before us, who are no longer alive. Our ancestors have taught our family members many things, and passed on their knowledge and wisdom to us. Our ancestor may have done nice things or left special possessions to our families, which we still have today. Today we are going to think about something we are thankful for that an ancestor gave to you or your family."

C. Thankful to Our Ancestors
1. Have the children close their eyes and think about an ancestor from their family and think about something that their ancestor gave them that they are thankful for (wisdom, knowledge, gift, etc) Let it out of your body.
2. Draw what they are thankful for on black paper using white chalk.
3. Share with class.

CLOSURE/ DISCUSSION

- How does that affect your life today?

- Take a moment of silence to thank that ancestor for this gift

Facilitator Manual Start Up! 123

WEEK 6

COMPLETE A PICTURE

TRANSFORMATION PHASE

Purpose:
Cognitive Homeostasis

Goal:
Understanding Past/Present and Reclaiming Self

Neural Activity:
Cerebrum

Benefits:
- Abstract Thinking
- Development of Imagination
- Cultivating Cultural Pride/Identity

Duration:
8 Weeks

Session 2 - Friday

ACTIVITY: COMPLETE A PICTURE

Art Materials:
- Markers
- 2 Piece each of 9 x 12 paper
- Cultural Photos
- Colored Pencils
- Glue Sticks

HEAD SHOULDERS KNEES & TOES

BREATHING / MEDITATION
"Close your eyes or leave them open if you would like. Breathe in deeply through your nose or mouth, until your lungs are full. Let your breath out until your lungs are empty. Imagine your mind is blank; there are no thoughts about problems or worries, or what you have to do today, etc. Let your mind be still and not have to work so hard. Listen to the sound of your own breath entering into your body. Feel the weight of your own body in your seat. Breathe for awhile and let your mind rest."

ART DIRECTIVES:

A. **Bi-Lateral Scribble:**

Two handed Marker drawing (1 Marker/crayon for each hand): Each movement is done for 9-10 seconds. We encourage the children to look at their marks on the paper, the teacher can stand at the front of the group and demonstrate on the chalkboard, describing the process of bilateral scribbling **(Younger children may need help with taping and movements at first):**

1. Tape Paper onto table (horizontally).
2. Make Random Marks with both hands.
3. Make Vertical Lines beginning from the bottom of the paper to the top, up and down. (can alternate hands).
4. Make Horizontal Lines, across paper with each hand on opposite edge of page," bringing their markers to meet in the middle. Have children cross the midline (cross arms to opposite sides of the paper and back to opposite side of page-repeat)
5. Make two Arcs, or windshield wiper movements, back and forth. Let the Arcs move into two large circles and go around and around.
6. Continue to make Circles in the reverse direction,- reverse again/ repeating.

COMPLETE A PICTURE

WEEK 6

A. Bi-Lateral Scribble Cont.:
7. Make gentle Dots- now go up and down on the paper, now back and forth across the paper.
8. Put one arm and hand over the other and make a Big X and now move the other arm and hand on top, now the other on top (repeat 4-5 times)
9. Make Fast Circles, go around really fast, now gradually slower and smaller, until you have a small circle add dot in the middle of the smallest circle, and STOP.

B. Bi-Lateral Drawing:
Flip paper and re-tape paper to table
With markers in each hand children are instructed to:
1. Draw a starry sky
2. Draw some star people (can add cultural teachings about traditional star knowledge beliefs of particular population)
3. Draw a spaceship
4. Draw a moon

MOTIVATION: "There are many beautiful animals, objects and people who come from each culture from around the world. Today we are going to choose an image from our own culture and complete it, using our imaginations."

C. Complete a Picture
1. Xerox a few different choices of cultural photos- neutral images from the culture, such as buffalo, tipi, warrior, day of the dead celebration, whale hunt, etc. Make sure image is incomplete, showing only partially the object.
2. Have children glue the image onto drawing paper leaving enough room to complete the drawing on the drawing paper. (Children will continue the lines from the photo and draw it onto the drawing paper). For younger children, have pre-glued images ready.
3. Share with class.

CLOSURE/ DISCUSSION

- Was it hard or easy?
- What did you like?
- What didn't you like?
- Did your picture relate to you or your life in any way?

Facilitator Manual Start Up! 125

WEEK 7 — SOMEONE YOU ADMIRE

TRANSFORMATION PHASE

Purpose:
Cognitive Homeostasis

Goal:
Understanding Past/Present and Reclaiming Self

Neural Activity:
Cerebrum

Benefits:
- Installation of Hope
- Identity Formation
- Emotional Expression

Duration:
8 Weeks

Session 1 - Monday

ACTIVITY: SOMEONE YOU ADMIRE

Art Materials:
- Markers
- 2 Pieces each of 9 x 12 paper
- Oil Pastels

MUSIC FREEZE

BREATHING / MEDITATION
"Close your eyes or leave them open if you really need to. Breathe in deeply through your nose or mouth, until your lungs are full. Let your breath out until your lungs are empty. Sit comfortably, feel feet on the ground. Breathe in and imagine a white light filling your body. Let it out. Imagine a color that represents your stress. Where in your body is this stress color? Breathe in the white light and let it take over your stress. Breathe out the stress color. Breathe in white light into your entire body, from your toes to the top of your head."

ART DIRECTIVES:

A. Bi-Lateral Scribble:
   Two handed Marker drawing (1 Marker/crayon for each hand): Each movement is done for 9-10 seconds. We encourage the children to look at their marks on the paper, the teacher can stand at the front of the group and demonstrate on the chalkboard, describing the process of bilateral scribbling **(Younger children may need help with taping and movements at first):**
  1. Tape Paper onto table (horizontally).
  2. Make Random Marks with both hands.
  3. Make Vertical Lines beginning from the bottom of the paper to the top, up and down. (can alternate hands).
  4. Make Horizontal Lines, across paper with each hand on opposite edge of page," bringing their markers to meet in the middle. Have children cross the midline (cross arms to opposite sides of the paper and back to opposite side of page-repeat)
  5. Make two Arcs, or windshield wiper movements, back and forth. Let the Arcs move into two large circles and go around and around.
  6. Continue to make Circles in the reverse direction,- reverse again/ repeating.

Start Up! — Facilitator Manual

SOMEONE YOU ADMIRE

WEEK 7

A. Bi-Lateral Scribble Cont.:
7. Make gentle Dots- now go up and down on the paper, now back and forth across the paper.
8. Put one arm and hand over the other and make a Big X and now move the other arm and hand on top, now the other on top (repeat 4-5 times)
9. Make Fast Circles, go around really fast, now gradually slower and smaller, until you have a small circle add dot in the middle of the smallest circle, and STOP.

B. Bi-Lateral Drawing:
Flip paper and re-tape paper to table
With markers in each hand children are instructed to:
1. Draw a waterline
2. Draw a boat (can be a traditional boat of particular population and add cultural teachings)
3. Draw a motor or sails to the boat (if applicable)
4. Draw a flag
5. Draw someone fishing with a line in the water with a hook
6. Draw some fish in the water
7. Add a shark
8. Draw a starfish in the water
9. Add clouds/sun/birds

MOTIVATION: "In our lives we have met people whom we admire. They may be people who have done great things; a tribal leader, a mentor, an activist, a president, your mother or father. Today we are going draw someone you admire. They can be real or imaginary; a superhero, world leader, or an elder from your culture.

C. Someone You Admire
1. Have the children close their eyes and take some deep breaths. Ask them to think of someone, real or imaginary whom they admire.
2. Ask the children to draw this person on a piece of drawing paper.
3. List 5 characteristics about that person you admire. List it on bottom or back.

CLOSURE/ DISCUSSION

- Was this hard or easy?

- Do any of the characteristics about the person you admire remind you of yourself or who you want to be?

- What did you notice about yourself today?

Facilitator Manual — Start Up!

WEEK 7

THE UGLIEST DRAWING

TRANSFORMATION PHASE

Purpose:
Cognitive Homeostasis

Goal:
Understanding Past/Present and Reclaiming Self

Neural Activity:
Cerebrum

Benefits:
- Development of Aesthetics
- Problem Solving
- Visual/Spatial Organization
- Transforming Negative to Positive

Duration:
8 Weeks

Session 2 - Friday

ACTIVITY: THE UGLIEST DRAWING

Art Materials:
- Markers
- 2 Pieces each of 9 x 12 paper
- Oil Pastels
- Pencil
- Ruler
- Scissors
- Glue Sticks
- 1 Piece Black Construction Paper

SIMON SAYS

BREATHING / MEDITATION
"Close your eyes or leave them open if you really would like. Breathe in deeply through your nose or mouth, until your lungs are full. Let your breath out until your lungs are empty. Sit comfortably, feel feet on the ground. Imagine a safe place; a place where you feel good, a place where you feel peace."

ART DIRECTIVES:

A. Bi-Lateral Scribble:

Two handed Marker drawing (1 Marker/crayon for each hand): Each movement is done for 9-10 seconds. We encourage the children to look at their marks on the paper, the teacher can stand at the front of the group and demonstrate on the chalkboard, describing the process of bilateral scribbling **(Younger children may need help with taping and movements at first):**

1. Tape Paper onto table (horizontally).
2. Make Random Marks with both hands.
3. Make Vertical Lines beginning from the bottom of the paper to the top, up and down. (can alternate hands).
4. Make Horizontal Lines, across paper with each hand on opposite edge of page," bringing their markers to meet in the middle. Have children cross the midline (cross arms to opposite sides of the paper and back to opposite side of page-repeat)
5. Make two Arcs, or windshield wiper movements, back and forth. Let the Arcs move into two large circles and go around and around.

THE UGLIEST DRAWING

WEEK 7

A. Bi-Lateral Scribble Cont.:
6. Continue to make Circles in the reverse direction,- reverse again/repeating.
7. Make gentle Dots- now go up and down on the paper, now back and forth across the paper.
8. Put one arm and hand over the other and make a Big X and now move the other arm and hand on top, now the other on top (repeat 4-5 times)
9. Make Fast Circles, go around really fast, now gradually slower and smaller, until you have a small circle add dot in the middle of the smallest circle, and STOP.

B. Bi-Lateral Drawing:
Flip paper and re-tape paper to table
With markers in each hand children are instructed to:
1. Draw a groundline
2. Draw a dinosaur (or animal special to traditions of particular population, buffalo, whale, jaguar, etc. Include cultural teachings of animal)
3. Draw tree
4. Draw a sun
5. Draw another animal

MOTIVATION: " Sometimes we are pleasantly surprised when we think something might not turn out very good and it ends up good. Sometimes we can make a bad feeling or bad situation good. Sometimes we can make something ugly into something beautiful, and that is what we are going to do today."

C. The Ugliest Drawing
1. Make the ugliest, messiest drawing you have ever seen with oil pastel on white paper.
2. Trace 7 small triangles out of that messy drawing.
3. Give each child a square of black construction paper.
4. Make a design with triangles, leaving a 1" border around all edges.
5. Glue them onto the black paper.
6. **Note:** For younger children help them cut triangles. Have a pre-drawn border drawn onto the black paper.

CLOSURE/ DISCUSSION

- Did you like the messy image before you cut it up?

- Do you like it now that the image is transformed into triangles on black paper?

- Did you think something ugly could be transformed into something beautiful?

Facilitator Manual Start Up! 129

WEEK 8

HONOR YOUR PAST / HONOR YOUR FUTURE

TRANSFORMATION PHASE

Purpose:
Cognitive Homeostasis

Goal:
Understanding Past/Present and Reclaiming Self

Neural Activity:
Cerebrum

Benefits:
• Identity Formation
• Abstract Thinking
• Self Expression
• Experience of Control
• Decision Making
• Transforming Negative to Positive

Duration:
8 Weeks

Session 1 - Monday

ACTIVITY: HONOR YOUR PAST / HONOR YOUR FUTURE

Art Materials:
• Markers
• 2 Pieces of 9 x 12 paper
• 1 Piece Colored Construction Paper
• Paint in Small Cups
• Brushes
• Water
• Towels
• Glue

HEAD SHOULDERS KNEES & TOES

BREATHING / MEDITATION
"Close your eyes or leave them open if you really need to. Breathe in deeply through your nose or mouth, until your lungs are full. Let your breath out until your lungs are empty. Imagine there is something you wish to let go of in your life. It might be an old habit, like waking up late for school, or using swear words, etc. Imagine putting whatever it is into a balloon and filling it up with air, then letting the balloon go. You watch the balloon float high into the sky until it disappears. Notice what it feels like in your body to have let go."

ART DIRECTIVES:
  A. **Bi-Lateral Scribble:**
   Two handed Marker drawing (1 Marker/crayon for each hand): Each movement is done for 9-10 seconds. We encourage the children to look at their marks on the paper, the teacher can stand at the front of the group and demonstrate on the chalkboard, describing the process of bilateral scribbling **(Younger children may need help with taping and movements at first):**
  1. Tape Paper onto table (horizontally).
  2. Make Random Marks with both hands.
  3. Make Vertical Lines beginning from the bottom of the paper to the top, up and down. (can alternate hands).
  4. Make Horizontal Lines, across paper with each hand on opposite edge of page," bringing their markers to meet in the middle. Have children cross the midline (cross arms to opposite sides of the paper and back to opposite side of page-repeat)
  5. Make two Arcs, or windshield wiper movements, back and forth. Let the Arcs move into two large circles and go around and around.

HONOR YOUR PAST / HONOR YOUR FUTURE — WEEK 8

A. Bi-Lateral Scribble Cont.:
6. Continue to make Circles in the reverse direction,- reverse again/ repeating.
7. Make gentle Dots- now go up and down on the paper, now back and forth across the paper.
8. Put one arm and hand over the other and make a Big X and now move the other arm and hand on top, now the other on top (repeat 4-5 times)
9. Make Fast Circles, go around really fast, now gradually slower and smaller, until you have a small circle add dot in the middle of the smallest circle, and STOP.

B. Bi-Lateral Drawing:
Flip paper and re-tape paper to table
With markers in each hand children are instructed to:
1. Draw a groundline
2. Draw some flowers
3. Draw some ladybugs
4. Draw some spiders
5. Draw some mosquitoes

MOTIVATION: "We all grow and learn as we get older, and learn from our mistakes. We are always learning better ways to deal and cope with difficult feelings and situations, but we aren't always perfect, and we might act in ways we don't want to act anymore. You might be thinking about letting go of old things and old ways of acting. Today we are going to do art about letting go of old things and old ways. It could be something you have said and done or things you didn't like, or forgive someone, or letting go of a way you used to think about yourself or someone else."

C. Honor Your Past / Honor your Future
1. Honor your past- make a painting of things you would like to let go of.
2. Honor the future- rip up your painting to symbolize letting it go and create new art piece to honor your next steps.
3. Glue the ripped up pieces onto colored construction paper.
4. Students can share if they choose.

CLOSURE/ DISCUSSION

- Describe what you learned about yourself?

- What does it feel like to let go of those things and know you have control of them?

WEEK 8

HONORING YOUR ANCESTORS AND ELDERS

TRANSFORMATION PHASE

Purpose:
Cognitive Homeostasis

Goal:
Understanding Past/Present and Reclaiming Self

Neural Activity:
Cerebrum

Benefits:
- Development of Imagination
- Installation of Hope
- Identity Formation
- Cultivating Cultural Pride/Identity

Duration:
8 Weeks

Session 2, Friday

ACTIVITY: HONORING YOUR ANCESTORS AND ELDERS

Art Materials:
- Markers
- 2 Piece each of 9 x 12 paper
- Oil Pastels
- Chalk Pastels
- Paint
- Brushes
- Water

MUSIC FREEZE

BREATHING / MEDITATION
"Close your eyes or leave them open if you would like. Breathe in deeply through your nose or mouth, until your lungs are full. Let your breath out until your lungs are empty. Sit comfortably, feel your feet on the ground. Imagine you are walking through a forest of trees. You come to a little creek and sit down. You notice a bunch of natural clay on the bank of the creek. You scoop some of this clay into your hand and begin to think of your ancestors and how they may have made something from this same clay at this same creek. You begin to sculpt the clay into an object to honor your ancestors. What is it that you make?"

ART DIRECTIVES:

A. Bi-Lateral Scribble:
  Two handed Marker drawing (1 Marker/crayon for each hand):
Each movement is done for 9-10 seconds. We encourage the children to look at their marks on the paper, the teacher can stand at the front of the group and demonstrate on the chalkboard, describing the process of bilateral scribbling **(Younger children may need help with taping and movements at first):**
  1. Tape Paper onto table (horizontally).
  2. Make Random Marks with both hands.
  3. Make Vertical Lines beginning from the bottom of the paper to the top, up and down. (can alternate hands).
  4. Make Horizontal Lines, across paper with each hand on opposite edge of page," bringing their markers to meet in the middle. Have children cross the midline (cross arms to opposite sides of the paper and back to opposite side of page-repeat)

HONORING YOUR ANCESTORS AND ELDERS

WEEK 8

A. Bi-Lateral Scribble Cont.:
5. Make two Arcs, or windshield wiper movements, back and forth. Let the Arcs move into two large circles and go around and around.
6. Continue to make Circles in the reverse direction,- reverse again/repeating.
7. Make gentle Dots- now go up and down on the paper, now back and forth across the paper.
8. Put one arm and hand over the other and make a Big X and now move the other arm and hand on top, now the other on top (repeat 4-5 times)
9. Make Fast Circles, go around really fast, now gradually slower and smaller, until you have a small circle add dot in the middle of the smallest circle, and STOP.

B. Bi-Lateral Drawing:
Flip paper and re-tape paper to table
With markers in each hand children are instructed to:
1. Draw a groundline
2. Draw a cactus
3. Draw a desert
4. Draw a skull
5. Draw another cactus
6. Draw a coyote
7. Draw a moon

MOTIVATION: "We have talked about ancestors before, who remembers what an ancestor is? Elders are similar, but they are older people in your family who are still alive. It might be your grandmother or grandfather or an Uncle or Aunt. Elders pass down their knowledge and wisdom, and teach us things. Your grandfather may have taught you to ride a horse, or build a canoe, depending on your culture, or your grandmother may have taught you to bead, or make the traditional arts of your people, or cook traditional foods. Your grandparents may have taught you how to cope with difficult situations. Today we are going to think of someone in your family who has been special to you and honor them by drawing or painting a picture of them. It doesn't have to look like them, just do your best. Stick figures are fine too."

C. Honor Your Ancestors and Elders
1. Make a drawing or painting of an ancestor or elder in your family.
2. Share with the class.

CLOSURE/ DISCUSSION

- Who did you honor?

- Is that something you strive to have in yourself?

- Is that something you would like to continue in your culture?

Congratulations!

You have completed the Transformation Phase, completing the third section of START UP!

You can decide if your class is ready to jump to the Integration Phase, or you can choose to start over in the Self Phase or repeat the Problem Phase or Transformation Phase. Remember: repetition reinforces, strengthens, and re-builds neural pathways, so it doesn't hurt to repeat activities.

Readiness to move to the Integration Phase is indicated by:

- Demonstrating development of a moral imperative; ability to know right from wrong (expressing guilt and regret).
- Taking responsibility and being accountable for behaviors.
- Improved problem-solving skills.
- Ability to define and articulate Self-Identity.
- Ability to regulate affect.
- Ability to articulate causal relationship between current emotional reactions and past experiences.
- Improved gross motor and motor planning skills.

THE INTEGRATION PHASE - 4 weeks

The following activities are designed to offer children safe and enjoyable activities that will promote development.

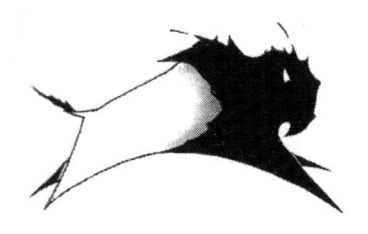

Objective

The Self Phase focused on physical homeostasis, the Problem Phase was centered on emotional homeostasis, and the Transformation Phase devoted to cognitive homeostasis. The Integration Phase is a culmination or *integration* of all phases or levels of the brain; activated and engaged. The Integration Phase is a synthesis of all systems working harmoniously, which is demonstrated in symptom reduction, a realistic and accurate concept of self, having adaptive coping strategies, and the ability to access creative expression and joy. It is within the Integration Phase that the frontal cortex is accessed to catalyze wisdom, empathy, compassion, sound decision-making, planning, and moral judgment.

By this time the child or teen has developed an affinity for the creative process. This is a time where continued exploration of the child's creative expression and imagination is highly encouraged, by not only using art to instill coping skills, but also for pleasure (Chapman, 2014). The Integration Phase is also a time for reviewing relationships, creating new boundaries, creating physical and psychological safety, and establishing a future orientation toward short and long-term goals. A major task of the Integration Phase of the Start Up! curriculum is to create new methods of coping, living, and relating to others (Chapman, 2014).

Because this is the completion of the Four Stage Trauma Treatment model, which the Start Up! curriculum is derived, it is important that the child or teen establish a strong support system. Therefore, they are encouraged to identify and engage these strong support systems as part of the completion of the year-long Start Up! curriculum within the classroom. Identifying and engaging a support system can be done by enlisting a trusted family member or other trusted adult to be available for assistance in, listening, comfort or problem-solving in times of stress (Chapman, 2014).

The goal of the Integration Phase is to continue and maintain the physical, emotional and cognitive homeostasis established in the previous phases of the Start Up! sessions, as well as the refinement of self-regulation and emotional processing.

The following chapter is devoted to providing Integration Phase activities which continue to build upon and improve the developmental achievements accomplished thus far, preparing the child and teen to be healthy, productive, and active members of society.

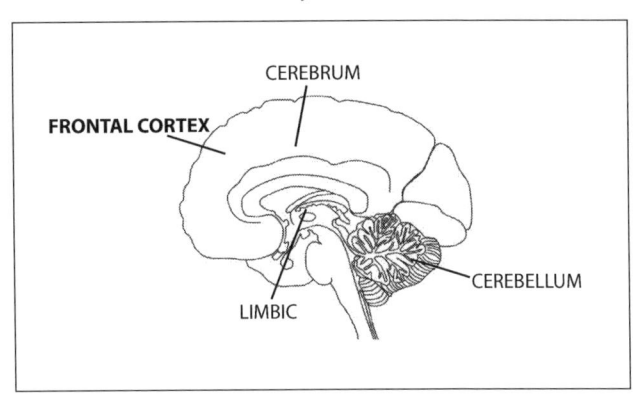

WEEK 1 — COLLAGE OF SUPPORT SYSTEM

INTEGRATION PHASE

Purpose:
Creativity

Goal:
Identity Support and Future Orientation

Neural Activity:
Frontal Cortex

Benefits:
- Identity Formation
- Developing Adaptive Coping Mechanisms
- Emotional Regulation

Duration:
4 Weeks

Session 1 - Monday

ACTIVITY: COLLAGE OF SUPPORT SYSTEM

Art Materials:
- Markers, (2 for each child)
- 1 Piece of 9x12 paper
- Construction Paper
- Scissors
- Gluesticks

SIMON SAYS

BREATHING / MEDITATION
"Close your eyes or leave them open if you would like. Breathe in deeply through your nose or mouth, until your lungs are full. Let your breath out until your lungs are empty. Keep your breath going strong. Think about ways you used to cope with difficult situations and how you deal with difficult situations now. Feel proud of yourself at how far you have come. Notice where in your body you feel your pride."

ART DIRECTIVES:

A. Bi-Lateral Scribble:
  Two handed Marker drawing (1 Marker/crayon for each hand): Each movement is done for 9-10 seconds. We encourage the children to look at their marks on the paper, the teacher can stand at the front of the group and demonstrate on the chalkboard, describing the process of bilateral scribbling **(Younger children may need help with taping and movements at first):**
  1. Tape Paper onto table (horizontally).
  2. Make Random Marks with both hands.
  3. Make Vertical Lines beginning from the bottom of the paper to the top, up and down. (can alternate hands).
  4. Make Horizontal Lines, across paper with each hand on opposite edge of page," bringing their markers to meet in the middle. Have children cross the midline (cross arms to opposite sides of the paper and back to opposite side of page-repeat)
  5. Make two Arcs, or windshield wiper movements, back and forth. Let the Arcs move into two large circles and go around and around.
  6. Continue to make Circles in the reverse direction,- reverse again/ repeating.

Start Up!

COLLAGE OF SUPPORT SYSTEM — WEEK 1

A. Bi-Lateral Scribble Cont.:
7. Make gentle Dots- now go up and down on the paper, now back and forth across the paper.
8. Put one arm and hand over the other and make a Big X and now move the other arm and hand on top, now the other on top (repeat 4-5 times)
9. Make Fast Circles, go around really fast, now gradually slower and smaller, until you have a small circle add dot in the middle of the smallest circle, and STOP.

B. Bi-Lateral Drawing:
Flip paper and re-tape paper to table
With markers in each hand children are instructed to:
1. Draw a groundline
2. Draw a house with windows and door (tipi, wigwam, hut, traditional home, can add cultural teachings about traditional homes of particular population)
3. Draw a tree
4. Draw a basket of apples underneath the tree (or can be traditional food and add cultural teachings about the traditional foods of
5. Put clouds up in the sky
6. Sun / Birds

MOTIVATION: "Who helps you when you are stressed? Who helps you when you are worried? It is important for everyone to have at least one trusted adult you can go to for comfort and advice. Who is this adult in your life? Who is your support system? If you do not have a support person, who would you like to have as your trusted adult?"

C. Collage Of Support System
1. Cut construction paper in the shape of a circle.
2. Cut out shapes/symbols from construction paper that represent supportive people or things for you. Supportive people might be an aunt/uncle, grandparents, parents, teachers, etc. Supportive things might include books, movies, music, art, etc.
3. Place shapes on the paper circle. Have children prioritize items in terms of what is most important(in the middle) to least important (on outer edge).
4. Glue shapes inside the paper circle.

CLOSURE/ DISCUSSION

- Which supportive person or thing is most important for you?

- Can you look and notice which one you use the most?

- Would you like to share with the group so we can all learn new ways of feeling supported?

- Does anyone have any new ways to share that hasn't been shared already?

WEEK 1　　　　　　　　　　　　　　　　　　　MY WORLD

INTEGRATION PHASE

Purpose:
Creativity

Goal:
Identity Support and Future Orientation

Neural Activity:
Frontal Cortex

Benefits:
• Identity Formation
•• Development of Imagination
•• Future Orientation
•• Opportunity for Choices
•• Building Self-Esteem

Duration:
4 Weeks

Session 2 - Friday

ACTIVITY: MY WORLD

Art Materials:
- Markers
- 2 Pieces of 9 x 12 paper
- Construction Paper
- Old Magazines
- Scissors
- Gluesticks

HEAD/SHOULDER/KNEES & TOES

BREATHING / MEDITATION
"Close your eyes or leave them open if you would like. Breathe in deeply through your nose or mouth, until your lungs are full. Let your breath out until your lungs are empty. Sit comfortably, feel feet on the ground. Think about some old behaviors or attitudes you have let go of. Now think about the new, healthier ways you behave, showing you are becoming more grown up. Feel proud of yourself. Feel joyful that you have succeeded in working so hard on yourself and have come so far. Take three more deep breaths and feel your joy."

ART DIRECTIVES:
A. Bi-Lateral Scribble:
   Two handed Marker drawing (1 Marker/crayon for each hand): Each movement is done for 9-10 seconds. We encourage the children to look at their marks on the paper, the teacher can stand at the front of the group and demonstrate on the chalkboard, describing the process of bilateral scribbling **(Younger children may need help with taping and movements at first):**
  1. Tape Paper onto table (horizontally).
  2. Make Random Marks with both hands.
  3. Make Vertical Lines beginning from the bottom of the paper to the top, up and down. (can alternate hands).
  4. Make Horizontal Lines, across paper with each hand on opposite edge of page," bringing their markers to meet in the middle. Have children cross the midline (cross arms to opposite sides of the paper and back to opposite side of page-repeat)
  5. Make two Arcs, or windshield wiper movements, back and forth. Let the Arcs move into two large circles and go around and around.
  6. Continue to make Circles in the reverse direction,- reverse again/ repeating.

MY WORLD — WEEK 1

A. Bi-Lateral Scribble Cont.:
7. Make gentle Dots- now go up and down on the paper, now back and forth across the paper.
8. Put one arm and hand over the other and make a Big X and now move the other arm and hand on top, now the other on top (repeat 4-5 times)
9. Make Fast Circles, go around really fast, now gradually slower and smaller, until you have a small circle add dot in the middle of the smallest circle, and STOP.

B. Bi-Lateral Drawing Cont.:
Flip paper and re-tape paper to table
With markers in each hand children are instructed to:
1. Draw a starry sky
2. Draw some star people (can add cultural teachings about traditional star knowledge beliefs of particular population)
3. Draw a spaceship
4. Draw a moon

C. Scribble Chase
1. Select a partner (each child has 1 marker)
2. Determine who will be the leader, the follower
3. Say "GO" and the leader leads with the marker and the follower tries to follow the leader on the paper with their marker (30-40 seconds each turn)
4. Switch roles

MOTIVATION: "Have you ever thought about your future and all the things you want and all the things you want to do in this world? Today we are going to create a collage called "My World."

D. My World
1. Have children cut out a circle from construction paper or use cake rounds (available on-line).
2. Have children cut out magazine images of everything they want in their world.
3. Place images within the paper circle.
4. Glue magazine images to circle to create a collage.
5. Share with the class.

CLOSURE/ DISCUSSION

- Look at your world, think about how you actually can have this if you play by the rules, and work hard. Would it be hard or easy to get this world?

- Take a moment and really imagine you are in that world… what would it feel like?

Facilitator Manual — Start Up! — 139

WEEK 2

BOUNDARY BOWLS

Session 1 - Monday

INTEGRATION PHASE

Purpose:
Creativity

Goal:
Identity Support and Future Orientation

Neural Activity:
Frontal Cortex

Benefits:
- Tactile Development
- Increase Ability to Delay Gratification

Duration:
4 Weeks

ACTIVITY: BOUNDARY BOWLS

Art Materials:
- Markers
- 1 Piece of 9x12 paper
- Balloons
- News Paper
- Mod Podge or School Glue
- Bowls

MUSIC FREEZE

BREATHING / MEDITATION
"Close your eyes or leave them open if you would like. Breathe in deeply through your nose or mouth, until your lungs are full. Let your breath out until your lungs are empty. Sit comfortably, feel your feet on the ground. Continue your breathing. Think of all the people in your life. You might feel very safe and comfortable with some people and other people you might not feel as comfortable and safe. Imagine yourself bringing the people you feel most safe with close to you and they form a circle around you. Imagine you pushing the people you do not feel as safe with to the outside of the circle. Feel this sense of safety from all the people in the circle around you. Take three deep breaths while feeling their safety."

ART DIRECTIVES:
  A. **Bi-Lateral Scribble:**
     Two handed Marker drawing (1 Marker/crayon for each hand): Each movement is done for 9-10 seconds. We encourage the children to look at their marks on the paper, the teacher can stand at the front of the group and demonstrate on the chalkboard, describing the process of bilateral scribbling **(Younger children may need help with taping and movements at first):**
   1. Tape Paper onto table (horizontally).
   2. Make Random Marks with both hands.
   3. Make Vertical Lines beginning from the bottom of the paper to the top, up and down. (can alternate hands).
   4. Make Horizontal Lines, across paper with each hand on opposite edge of page," bringing their markers to meet in the middle. Have children cross the midline (cross arms to opposite sides of the paper and back to opposite side of page-repeat)
   5. Make two Arcs, or windshield wiper movements, back and forth. Let the Arcs move into two large circles and go around and around.

Start Up! Facilitator Manual

BOUNDARY BOWLS

WEEK 2

A. Bi-Lateral Scribble Cont.:

6. Continue to make Circles in the reverse direction,- reverse again/ repeating.
7. Make gentle Dots- now go up and down on the paper, now back and forth across the paper.
8. Put one arm and hand over the other and make a Big X and now move the other arm and hand on top, now the other on top (repeat 4-5 times)
9. Make Fast Circles, go around really fast, now gradually slower and smaller, until you have a small circle add dot in the middle of the smallest circle, and STOP.

B. Bi-Lateral Drawing:

Flip paper and re-tape paper to table
With markers in each hand children are instructed to:
0) Draw a waterline
1. Draw a boat (can be a traditional boat of particular population and add cultural teachings)
2. Draw a motor or sails to the boat (if applicable)
3. Draw a flag
4. Draw someone fishing with a line in the water with a hook
5. Draw some fish in the water
6. Add a shark
7. Draw a starfish in the water
8. Add clouds/sun/birds
9. TEACHER- If you are a people originated near water, include cultural traditions and stories of water.

MOTIVATION: "Have you ever felt uncomfortable around strangers or even people you know? Have you ever gotten upset with a friend because they did something that wasn't nice? We all have people like this in our lives and sometimes we need to create boundaries with these people or maybe even end friendships. It is important to let people know what it is you need to feel safe. This is called boundaries. Boundaries are kind of like our own rules that others need to follow in order for you to feel safe. Today we are going to make Boundary Bowls."

C. Boundary Bowls

1. Have children blow up small balloons.
2. Have children dip newspaper strips into school glue or mod podge and cover bottom half of balloon. Repeat for 3-4 layers.
3. **Teacher: With younger children, you may want to have balloons already blown up, or pre-made bowls.**
4. Let Dry.

CLOSURE/ DISCUSSION

- How was it to do something that was kind of boring?

- How was it to do something challenging?

- How do you feel now that you have done something beyond you comfort zone?

Facilitator Manual — Start Up!

WEEK 2

BOUNDARY BOWLS - continued

INTEGRATION PHASE

Purpose:
Creativity

Goal:
Identity Support and Future Orientation

Neural Activity:
Frontal Cortex

Benefits:
- Experience of Control
- Creating Safety
- Opportunity for Choices
- Promotes Critical Thinking

Duration:
4 Weeks

Session 2 - Friday

ACTIVITY: BOUNDARY BOWLS - continued

Art Materials:
- Markers
- Sharp object to pop balloon
- Cups of paint
- Old magazines
- Scissors
- Gluesticks

SIMON SAYS

BREATHING / MEDITATION
"Close your eyes or leave them open if you would like. Breathe in deeply through your nose or mouth, until your lungs are full. Let your breath out until your lungs are empty. Think about ways that your give to your friends and family that feel good to you (maybe you are a good listener, or good babysitter, or like to cook for people). Think about ways you give to others that do not feel good to you (sometimes you might give to others a lot and you feel they do not give back to you in ways that feel good). Imagine putting up a boundary with those people that allows you to only give in the ways that feel good to you. You might imagine yourself telling a friend that you're unavailable to listen to their problems if you feel they never listen to your problems, or letting others know you aren't available to babysit if you feel you are not being paid or valued for your time, or you might cook less for others if you feel you are the one always cooking. Putting boundaries up helps you to feel empowered and in control of your needs. Take 3 deep breaths to feel what it is like to put boundaries up with people."

ART DIRECTIVES:

A. Bi-Lateral Scribble:
  Two handed Marker drawing (1 Marker/crayon for each hand):
Each movement is done for 9-10 seconds. We encourage the children to look at their marks on the paper, the teacher can stand at the front of the group and demonstrate on the chalkboard, describing the process of bilateral scribbling **(Younger children may need help with taping and movements at first):**
  1. Tape Paper onto table (horizontally).
  2. Make Random Marks with both hands.
  3. Make Vertical Lines beginning from the bottom of the paper to the top, up and down. (can alternate hands).
  4. Make Horizontal Lines, across paper with each hand on opposite edge of page," bringing their markers to meet in the middle. Have children cross the midline (cross arms to opposite sides of the paper and back to opposite side of page-repeat)

Start Up! Facilitator Manual

BOUNDARY BOWLS - continued

WEEK 2

A. Bi-Lateral Scribble Cont.:
5. Make two Arcs, or windshield wiper movements, back and forth. Let the Arcs move into two large circles and go around and around.
6. Continue to make Circles in the reverse direction,- reverse again/ repeating.
7. Make gentle Dots- now go up and down on the paper, now back and forth across the paper.
8. Put one arm and hand over the other and make a Big X and now move the other arm and hand on top, now the other on top (repeat 4-5 times)
9. Make Fast Circles, go around really fast, now gradually slower and smaller, until you have a small circle add dot in the middle of the smallest circle, and STOP.

B. Bi-Lateral Drawing:
Flip paper and re-tape paper to table.
With markers in each hand children are instructed to:
1. Draw underground
2. Draw a snake underground
3. Draw a family of snakes underground
4. Draw a prairie dog underground
5. Draw a fox
6. Draw a rabbit
7. Add a family of rabbits
8. Draw some ants
9. Add clouds/sun/birds above ground

MOTIVATION: "Boundaries are very important. We have talked about what boundaries are before. Can anyone tell me a time when you had to put up a boundary with someone? (Let the children share). Today we are going to finish our boundary bowls that we started last week."

C. Boundary Bowls - continued
1. Pop the balloon with a sharp object (pen, pencil, paperclip) and remove.
2. Paint your bowl any colors you would like.
3. ON THE OUTSIDE OF THE BOWL: Cut out images from magazines representing your boundaries or things you don't like from other people; words, things, behavior. Glue these images onto THE OUTSIDE of your bowl.
4. ON THE INSIDE OF YOUR BOWL: What things do you have to give and share if you choose (not what people take): I am a good babysitter, music, I am a good friend, listener, cook, etc. Cut out images that reflect this and glue them on THE INSIDE of your bowl.
5. Sharing is optional.

CLOSURE/ DISCUSSION

- What things do you have to give and share?

- How did it feel to know you do not have to give these things?

WEEK 3

CREATE A RAINBOW

INTEGRATION PHASE

Purpose:
Creativity

Goal:
Identity Support and Future Orientation

Neural Activity:
Frontal Cortex

Benefits:
- Teaches Color and Composition
- Broadens Intellectual Repertoire of Concepts
- Development of Abstract Thinking
- Future Orientation

Duration:
4 Weeks

Session 1 - Monday

ACTIVITY: CREATE A RAINBOW

Art Materials:
- Markers
- 1 Piece each of 9x12 paper
- 1 Piece of heavy duty paper
- Paint in small cups (red, blue, yellow)
- Brushes (medium sized)
- Extra paper for pallette

HEAD SHOULDERS KNEES AND TOES

BREATHING / MEDITATION

"Close your eyes or leave them open if you would like. Breathe in deeply through your nose or mouth, until your lungs are full. Let your breath out until your lungs are empty. Sit comfortably, feel your feet on the ground. Imagine yourself standing before a big piece of paper that covers an entire wall. You look down and see many containers of paint, more than you can count, in every color you can imagine. This blank paper is your future and you can paint anything you would like for your future on this paper. Imagine you pick up a brush and dip it in a color and start to paint. You dip your brush into another color and continue to paint. What does it look like when it is complete? Look at your image and now you can make this come true for yourself with hard work and following rules. Take 3 more deep breaths, then gently open your eyes."

ART DIRECTIVES:

  A. Bi-Lateral Scribble:

    Two handed Marker drawing (1 Marker/crayon for each hand): Each movement is done for 9-10 seconds. We encourage the children to look at their marks on the paper, the teacher can stand at the front of the group and demonstrate on the chalkboard, describing the process of bilateral scribbling **(Younger children may need help with taping and movements at first):**

1. Tape Paper onto table (horizontally).
2. Make Random Marks with both hands.
3. Make Vertical Lines beginning from the bottom of the paper to the top, up and down. (can alternate hands).
4. Make Horizontal Lines, across paper with each hand on opposite edge of page," bringing their markers to meet in the middle. Have children cross the midline (cross arms to opposite sides of the paper and back to opposite side of page-repeat)
5. Make two Arcs, or windshield wiper movements, back and forth. Let the Arcs move into two large circles and go around and around.

Start Up!   Facilitator Manual

CREATE A RAINBOW

WEEK 3

A. Bi-Lateral Scribble Cont.:
6. Continue to make Circles in the reverse direction,- reverse again/ repeating.
7. Make gentle Dots- now go up and down on the paper, now back and forth across the paper.
8. Put one arm and hand over the other and make a Big X and now move the other arm and hand on top, now the other on top (repeat 4-5 times)
9. Make Fast Circles, go around really fast, now gradually slower and smaller, until you have a small circle add dot in the middle of the smallest circle, and STOP.

B. Bi-Lateral Drawing:
Flip paper and re-tape paper to table
With markers in each hand children are instructed to:
1. Draw a groundline
2. Draw a dinosaur (or animal special to traditions of particular population, buffalo, whale, jaguar, etc. Include cultural teachings of animal)
3. Draw tree
4. Draw a sun
5. Draw another animal

MOTIVATION: "Did you know that every color of the rainbow comes from 3 colors called the primary colors, which are red, yellow, and blue. Some say the rainbow is a symbol of everlasting life or it symbolizes peace. Each culture has there own meaning of what rainbows mean to them; Native Americans, Asians, South Americans, Hawaiians, Caucasians, Africans, etc. What does the rainbow represent to you? Today we are going to paint our own rainbows."

C. Create a Rainbow
1. Have an example of a rainbow hanging at the front of the classroom.
2. Give each one a Dixie cup of each color (red, blue, yellow) and a brush and water.
3. Mix colors (from primary colors) together. Red +yellow= orange; yellow+ blue= green, blue+ red= purple. (Can use extra paper for pallete to mix colors.)
4. Have each child create their own rainbow.
5. **Teacher: "The Irish say there is a pot of gold at the end of the rainbow. What does the rainbow represent to you? What's at the end of your rainbow? Something in your future you want that is waiting for you at the end of your rainbow. You can paint it in if you wish."**
6. Have children experiment with making additional colors.
7. Share with class.

CLOSURE/ DISCUSSION

- What did you like most? Least?
- Was this hard or easy?
- What did you learn about yourself today?

WEEK 3

MANDALAS

INTEGRATION PHASE

Purpose:
Creativity

Goal:
Identity Support and Future Orientation

Neural Activity:
Frontal Cortex

Benefits:
- Community Building
- Environmental Awareness
- Identity Formation

Duration:
4 Weeks

Session 2, Friday

ACTIVITY: MANDALAS

Art Materials:
- Markers
- 1 Piece each of 9x12 paper
- Large craft paper
- OR Construction paper
- Glue
- OR Sidewalk chalk
- OR Objects from nature (leaves, sticks, grasses, etc.)
- Oil/Chalk Pastels

MUSIC FREEZE

BREATHING / MEDITATION
"Close your eyes or leave them open if you really need to. Breathe in deeply through your nose or mouth, until your lungs are full. Let your breath out until your lungs are empty. Sit comfortably, feel your feet on the ground. Breathe in and imagine a white light filling your body. Let it out. Imagine yourself within a circle of light. You are in the center of this circle. Here you feel calm, peaceful, and whole. What color is your circle of light? Imagine this circle of light is protecting you. Take a few deep breaths here"

ART DIRECTIVES:

A. Bi-Lateral Scribble:

Two handed Marker drawing (1 Marker/crayon for each hand): Each movement is done for 9-10 seconds. We encourage the children to look at their marks on the paper, the teacher can stand at the front of the group and demonstrate on the chalkboard, describing the process of bilateral scribbling **(Younger children may need help with taping and movements at first):**

1. Tape Paper onto table (horizontally).
2. Make Random Marks with both hands.
3. Make Vertical Lines beginning from the bottom of the paper to the top, up and down. (can alternate hands).
4. Make Horizontal Lines, across paper with each hand on opposite edge of page," bringing their markers to meet in the middle. Have children cross the midline (cross arms to opposite sides of the paper and back to opposite side of page-repeat)
5. Make two Arcs, or windshield wiper movements, back and forth. Let the Arcs move into two large circles and go around and around.
6. Continue to make Circles in the reverse direction,- reverse again/ repeating.

MANDALAS

WEEK 3

A. Bi-Lateral Scribble Cont.:
7. Make gentle Dots- now go up and down on the paper, now back and forth across the paper.
8. Put one arm and hand over the other and make a Big X and now move the other arm and hand on top, now the other on top (repeat 4-5 times)
9. Make Fast Circles, go around really fast, now gradually slower and smaller, until you have a small circle add dot in the middle of the smallest circle, and STOP.

B. Bi-Lateral Drawing:
Flip paper and re-tape paper to table
With markers in each hand children are instructed to:
1. Draw a groundline
2. Draw a desert
3. Draw a cactus
4. Draw a tumbleweed
5. Draw a lizard
6. Draw a big rock
7. Draw a vulture in the sky
8. Teacher- You can include traditions and stories of Desert Tribes; diet, how they obtained water, etc

MOTIVATION: "The word mandala means "circle" and comes from the people of India. To them the mandala represents wholeness. Who knows what wholeness means? Many cultures around the world use the circle as a symbol which represents something different to each culture. Native Americans use the medicine wheel to represent the directions, or the the Sacred Hoop, where all things are connected; there is no beginning and no end. For many other cultures the circle also meant there is no beginning and no end, that we are all connected as One. What are some ideas that the circle or mandala might mean to you? Today we are going to break into groups and make group mandalas." (Show example from internet.)

C. Mandalas
1. Decide if you will be making your mandalas in one of 3 ways: On large craft paper with markers/pastels, OR on large craft paper with objects from nature, OR on the playground with sidewalk chalk.
2. If making mandalas on large craft paper, have pre-cut large circles from large craft paper ready. If making mandalas on the playground, have re-traced circles drawn on the ground.
3. Have an example of a mandala large enough for the class to see. Have each group talk about which shapes they would like to begin with and think of a design. Draw or make mandalas.
4. "Pay attention to how you feel while you are making your mandala. Do you feel whole? Do you feel connected with your group?"
5. Share with class.

CLOSURE/ DISCUSSION

- What was your role in the group?
- Were you a leader, follower, designer?
- What role were you most comfortable in?
- Are you more of a doer or like to watch?

WEEK 4

RESPONSE ART

INTEGRATION PHASE

Purpose:
Creativity

Goal:
Identity Support and Future Orientation

Neural Activity:
Frontal Cortex

Benefits:
- Development of Abstract Thinking
- Identity Formation
- Delaying Gratification
- Patience
- Broadening Repertoire of Intellectual Concepts

Duration:
4 Weeks

Session 1 - Monday

ACTIVITY: RESPONSE ART

Art Materials:
- Markers
- 1 Piece each of 9x12 paper
- Model Magic Clay- 1 pkg each

SIMON SAYS

BREATHING / MEDITATION
"Close your eyes or leave them open if you would like. Breathe in deeply through your nose or mouth, until your lungs are full. Let your breath out until your lungs are empty. You are all very good at meditation by now so today we will try to go for our record time and see how long we can do it."

ART DIRECTIVES:
A. Bi-Lateral Scribble:
   Two handed Marker drawing (1 Marker/crayon for each hand): Each movement is done for 9-10 seconds. We encourage the children to look at their marks on the paper, the teacher can stand at the front of the group and demonstrate on the chalkboard, describing the process of bilateral scribbling **(Younger children may need help with taping and movements at first):**
  1. Tape Paper onto table (horizontally).
  2. Make Random Marks with both hands.
  3. Make Vertical Lines beginning from the bottom of the paper to the top, up and down. (can alternate hands).
  4. Make Horizontal Lines, across paper with each hand on opposite edge of page," bringing their markers to meet in the middle. Have children cross the midline (cross arms to opposite sides of the paper and back to opposite side of page-repeat)
  5. Make two Arcs, or windshield wiper movements, back and forth. Let the Arcs move into two large circles and go around and around.
  6. Continue to make Circles in the reverse direction,- reverse again/ repeating.

RESPONSE ART
WEEK 4

A. Bi-Lateral Scribble Cont.:
7. Make gentle Dots- now go up and down on the paper, now back and forth across the paper.
8. Put one arm and hand over the other and make a Big X and now move the other arm and hand on top, now the other on top (repeat 4-5 times)
9. Make Fast Circles, go around really fast, now gradually slower and smaller, until you have a small circle add dot in the middle of the smallest circle, and STOP.

B. Bi-Lateral Drawing:
Flip paper and re-tape paper to table
With markers in each hand children are instructed to:
1. Draw a groundline
2. Draw favorite animal
3. Draw tree
4. Draw a sun
5. Draw another animal of same type

MOTIVATION: "We have been making art together twice a week for the whole school year. We have learned many things about ourselves, and each other. We have learned healthy coping skills and how to work as a group. We have identified support systems for ourselves and created goals for our futures. How does it feel when thinking about all the things we have covered through our artmaking? Today we are going to make a sculpture in response to how we feel about all we have learned through the Start Up! program this year."

C. Response Art
1. Give each child a package of Model Magic.
2. "Sculpt something that represents how this art process has been for you, and why you like art?"
3. Let sculptures dry until next session.

CLOSURE/ DISCUSSION

- Why do you like art?

- How have you benefitted most from art?

- How is art important in your culture?

- How does art benefit your culture?

WEEK 4

RESPONSE ART-continued

INTEGRATION PHASE

Purpose:
Creativity

Goal:
Identity Support and Future Orientation

Neural Activity:
Frontal Cortex

Benefits:
- Community Building
- Building Adaptive Coping Mechanisms
- Emotional Expression

Duration:
4 Weeks

Session 2 - Friday

ACTIVITY: RESPONSE ART-continued

Art Materials:
- Markers, (2 for each child)
- 1 Piece each of 9x12 paper
- Paint
- Brushes
- Water
- Feathers, glitter, yarn, pompoms, etc
- Glue

HEAD SHOULDERS KNEES & TOES

BREATHING / MEDITATION
"Close your eyes or leave them open if you would like. Breathe in deeply through your nose or mouth, until your lungs are full. Let your breath out until your lungs are empty. Last session, we went for our record meditation time. We were able to go for _____ minutes! Today we are going to see if we can beat that record. Keep your eyes closed and your body and mind rested. Let's see how long we can go for today."

ART DIRECTIVES:
A. Bi-Lateral Scribble:
   Two handed Marker drawing (1 Marker/crayon for each hand):
Each movement is done for 9-10 seconds. We encourage the children to look at their marks on the paper, the teacher can stand at the front of the group and demonstrate on the chalkboard, describing the process of bilateral scribbling **(Younger children may need help with taping and movements at first):**
1. Tape Paper onto table (horizontally).
2. Make Random Marks with both hands.
3. Make Vertical Lines beginning from the bottom of the paper to the top, up and down. (can alternate hands).
4. Make Horizontal Lines, across paper with each hand on opposite edge of page," bringing their markers to meet in the middle. Have children cross the midline (cross arms to opposite sides of the paper and back to opposite side of page-repeat)
5. Make two Arcs, or windshield wiper movements, back and forth. Let the Arcs move into two large circles and go around and around.
6. Continue to make Circles in the reverse direction,- reverse again/ repeating.

RESPONSE ART-continued

WEEK 4

A. Bi-Lateral Scribble Cont.:
A. Bi-Lateral Scribble:

7. Make gentle Dots- now go up and down on the paper, now back and forth across the paper.
8. Put one arm and hand over the other and make a Big X and now move the other arm and hand on top, now the other on top (repeat 4-5 times)
9. Make Fast Circles, go around really fast, now gradually slower and smaller, until you have a small circle add dot in the middle of the smallest circle, and STOP.

B. Bi-Lateral Drawing:
Flip paper and re-tape paper to table
With markers in each hand children are instructed to:
1. Draw a sky
2. Draw a moon
3. Draw stars
4. Draw planets
5. Draw a spaceship
6. Draw a star being (alien)

MOTIVATION: "Like we talked about last time, through making art together, we have learned so much about ourselves, and each other. We have learned healthy coping skills and how to work as a group. We have identified support systems for ourselves and created goals for our futures. How does it feel when thinking about all the things we have covered through our art making? This knowledge is in your minds and in your hearts, and you can take this home with you and use it during the summer. You will have this for the rest of your life, so practice these lessons and get good at it. Today we are going to paint our sculptures."

C. Responsive Art - continued
1. Give children paint in cups, brushes.
2. Have children choose objects to embellish sculpture.
3. Play soft cultural music.
4. **Teacher: Burn sage, copal, palo santo, etc. to purify the sculptures as a symbol of new beginnings.**
5. Share with class.

CLOSURE/ DISCUSSION

- What did you learn about yourself through the Start Up! Program this year?

- How can you remember your coping skills and boundaries over the summer?

- What coping skills do you think you might use the most over summer?

- What boundaries do you think you will use the most this year?

Congratulations!

You have completed the Integration Phase, completing the entire START UP! curriculum!

You have guided your students through a sequential process, engaging in art activities, corresponding to the lower structures of the brain, to the higher structure of the brain.

Completion of the Integration Phase and the START UP! curriculum is an accomplishment. Your students will continue to improve upon the accomplishments made in the Transformation Phase, as well as accomplish additional goals.

Additional Accomplishments from Integration Phase:

- Developed affinity for the creative process for pleasure.
- Reviewing relationships.
- Creating new boundaries.
- Creating physical and psychological safety.
- Establishing a future orientation toward short and long-term goals.
- Create new methods of coping, living, and relating to others.
- Identify and engage strong support systems.

CONCLUSION

Learning in the classroom continues to be problematic for many children. Children who have difficulty sitting still are often labeled as hyperactive. Those who cannot sit upright are often told they are lazy. Those who cannot process information are accused of not listening. Little attention is paid to the importance of developmental assessments to determine developmental sensitivities and delays that can cause significant problems for children, youth and adults. Developmental sensitivities and delays can often appear as symptoms of mental health disorders, and treating the mental health disorder is often the first approach to treatment.

Access to services is a hardship for many families due to finances, transportation, time, and child care needs. The START UP! Curriculum offers services to children in a cost effective, timely manner, with low fiscal impact on the schools. It is our hope that these activities will alleviate information processing sensitivities and delays early in development to allow the children ease with learning, social interaction, and self-confidence and self-worth.

Lastly, there is little time in a child's life for creativity, art making, music, and other life enhancing experiences. Giving the children and youth the opportunity for creative endeavors creates the mind/body concept of Self. And, the experiences are fun and enlivening, a wonderful way to start the school day!

For questions and Start Up! training information, please contact:

Carey MacCarthy, MA, ATR-LPCC #473
Founder/Executive Director, Indigenous Healing Arts Alliance
10 Santa Margarita Dr
San Rafael CA 94901
415-947-9608
carey@indigenoushealingarts.org
Indigenoushealingarts.org

For questions on Neurodevelopemental Art Therapy, please contact:

Linda Chapman, MA, ATR-BC
Founder/ Executive Director, Art Therapy Institute of The Redwoods
10151 East Road
Redwood Valley, CA 95470
707-485-0105
arttherapy@pacific.net

REFERENCES

Chapman, L. (2014.) Neurobiologically Informed Trauma Therapy with Children and Adolescents: Understanding Mechanisms of Change. NY: Norton.

Perry, B. (1995). Incubated in Terror: Neurodevelopmental Factors in the 'Cycle of Violence'. In Children, Youth and Violence: Searching for Solutions. New York: Guilford Press.

Schore, A.N. (2012). The Science of the Art of Psychotherapy. NY: Norton.

Made in the USA
Middletown, DE
18 May 2022